Malcolm Guite is the chaplain of Girton College, Cambridge and teaches for the Cambridge Federation of Theological Colleges. He is a published poet and the singer/songwriter for the band Mystery Train. He lives near Cambridge with his wife and two children.

Also available

What Do Buddhists Believe? Tony Morris
What Do Muslims Believe? Ziauddin Sardar
What Do Jews Believe? Edward Kessler

What Do
CHRISTIANS
Believe?

Belonging and Belief in Modern Christianity

Malcolm Guite

Walker & Company
New York

Published by Walker Publishing Company, Inc., New York
Distributed to the trade by Macmillan

All papers used by Walker & Company are natural, recyclable products
made from wood grown in well-managed forests. The manufacturing
processes conform to the environmental regulations of the country of origin.

LIBRARY OF CONGRESS CATALOGING-IN-PUBLICATION DATA HAS BEEN
APPLIED FOR

ISBN-10: 0-8027-1640-7
ISBN-13: 978-0-8027-1640-8

Visit Walker & Company's Web site at www.walkerbooks.com

First published in the United Kingdom by Granta Books in 2006
First U.S. Edition 2008

1 3 5 7 9 10 8 6 4 2

Typeset by M Rules
Printed in the United States of America by Quebecor World Fairfield

In Memoriam
H. F. Guite, scholar and preacher

Contents

Acknowledgements

I have benefited enormously from the conversation and correspondence of Christian friends in many denominations in preparing this book. Romie Ridley kindly read the manuscript and made many helpful suggestions. I have been grateful for patience from my editors and encouragement from my wife.

Chronology

0AD	Jesus *c.*4 BC–AD 30
	Paul's Missions and letters *c.*50–60
100	Gospels written *c.*70–95
200	
300	Constantine emperor 306–337
301	Canon of New Testament set 367
	St Augustine 354–430
	Fall of Rome 410
400	St Benedict 480–542 first monasticism
	(Birth of Mohammed *c.*570)
500	
600	(written text of Koran established 650)
700	Orthodoxy reaches Russia, Latin Christianity meets with Celtic Christianity in England Synod of Whitby 664
800	
900	
1000	Split between Western and Eastern Orthodox church 1054
1100	Crusades 1095–1350
1200	St Francis of Assisi 1182–1226

1300	Development of monastic orders, building of Cathedrals, St Thomas Aquinas 1225–74, Dante 1265–1321
1400	(Constantinople captured for Islam, renamed Istanbul 1453)
1500	Luther publishes 95 theses calling for reformation 1517, Protestant reformation underway. 1545–63 Council of Trent Roman Catholic reformation. 1534 Church of England separates from Rome
1600	Missions to New World, worldwide expansion of Christianity
1700	Enlightenment movement in Europe challenges many traditional teachings, gives birth to both a more liberal interpretation of scripture and, in reaction, a more literal fundamentalism
1800	
1900	World Council of Churches formed 1948. Freedom of religion comes to USSR and eastern bloc post-1989. Mother Theresa 1910–97
2000	

1

What is a Christian?

Belonging, believing and behaving

Christianity began as a minor sect within Judaism and has now become one of the major world religions with nearly two billion adherents spread across every nation on earth. It began with a small group of people who shared the same language, lifestyle and background. It now embraces many languages and cultures, giving rise to an astonishing variety of practices and interpretations, yet all with a common basis of shared faith inspired by the teaching, life, death and new life of a carpenter from Nazareth. How has this happened? How do the events that changed the life of Jesus' first disciples continue to release such power in people's lives, be they Copts in Egypt, members of the Orthodox church in Russia, Baptists in America or Anglicans in an English village?

For all the differences in tradition, in emphasis and in understanding, we can identify three core elements which are essential parts of what it means to be a Christian. The first is a sense of *belonging*. Not simply of being a person who, in the words of the old prayer book, 'professes and calls themselves' a Christian, though that is part of it. Deeper than that, is the sense of belonging in a faith-community. Christianity is not a private or cerebral religion. It has community and belonging at its core. The earliest Christian documents show that Jesus' first followers belonged so closely to one another that they regarded themselves as a single body. Jesus is described as promising to be with future Christians not solely in private prayer or meditation but 'wherever two or three are gathered together in my name'. Finally, the sense of belonging is intrinsic to the meaning of being Christian because Christians believe that they belong not only to one another but also to God. With that ultimate sense of belonging comes a shadow and fugitive sense of *not belonging*, of not belonging entirely to this world, to the appetites of the body or even to the apparently final claims of death. From this paradox, of belonging and not belonging, arises the characteristic quality of Christian mystic life and prayer which is simply *longing*, yearning for the beyond, the final, transcendent encounter with God where they will belong and all other longing will be fulfilled.

Believing is the second essential characteristic of being a Christian. It arises within the community of belonging. Members of that community acquire and eventually inhabit a system of belief and a framework of faith about the pivotal role of Jesus as the meeting place of God and humanity, the person in whom a broken relationship is restored. These beliefs have been differently expressed and emphasized by different Christian communities. Sometimes these differences have been so great as to break the bonds of belonging in which they were first nurtured, leading to schism and even to religious warfare. These historic splits and conflicts by their very nature undermined the beliefs they purported to defend. Nevertheless, as we will see, there are still core beliefs to which almost all Christian communities in all ages have continued to bear witness.

The third common element in being Christian is an emphasis on *behaving*. Christianity has at its core a sense that human behaviour is significant, indeed that it has eternal significance. What we *do* is both the consequence and the cause of what we *are*. Christians believe that there are choices between good and evil, and that the ultimate arbiter of these choices should be Love. This is not to say that Christians are unanimous about what constitutes loving behaviour, or even about how far distinctive behaviour, or 'sanctified living', is an essential or qualifying element of 'being' a Christian. But all would agree that the Christian faith could never be indifferent to the way we actually live.

So, if the three essential elements of 'being a Christian' are belonging, believing and behaving, what is the relation between them? Which has priority? Would we still recognize as Christian a person or community in whom one of these elements was lacking or severely weakened? In answering these questions we can immediately identify the differences between Christians.

At any period in history you can find a community that has emphasized one of these three at the expense of the others. These differences of emphasis do not simply follow the lines of historic division between Catholic, Protestant and Orthodox, or even the sectarian divisions into denominations within Protestantism (see below, p. 53–4). Rather, they are differences of style, tone and emphasis found within each different denomination.

Any one of these elements, emphasized at the expense of the other two, can lead to distortions which damage both believers and those with whom they interact. A Church that emphasizes mere *belonging* in isolation from belief and behaviour easily becomes tribal and chauvinistic. Christianity becomes conflated with race or nation. It becomes a badge of identity, which neither challenges behaviour nor reflects the core beliefs and teachings of its founder. The history of Christian Europe is littered with sad examples, from the expulsion of Jews from Catholic Spain in the Middle Ages to the massacre of Muslims by 'orthodox' Serbian Christians in Srebrenica just ten years ago.

A Church that emphasizes *belief* and absolute purity of doctrine as a condition of belonging, independent of behaviour, swiftly becomes fundamentalist and sectarian. In such a Church only those who assent to an exact definition and refuse to question or explore are counted as 'true Christians'. The Church becomes preoccupied with potential schisms and internal heresy hunts while the 'purity' of official doctrine often masks hypocrisy and mere power-play. The current resurgence of some forms of Christian fundamentalism often betrays these tendencies.

A Church that only emphasizes the Christian moral imperatives in the commandments, and the call to radical holiness of living, can end up instituting a soul-sapping legalism, promoting the idea that it is necessary to 'keep all the rules' to obtain salvation – an idea which Paul and other early Christian writers strongly rejected. Such Churches can present Christianity as a kind of spiritual athletics possible only to a few dedicated saints living the religious life, and dismiss the rest of humanity as tainted and defeated.

Like the persons of the Holy Trinity (see below, p. 75–7), these three aspects of being Christian are in reality interdependent and mutually sustaining. Belonging to a community involves both acquiring and inhabiting shared beliefs and acknowledging some corporate sense of the ideals of behaviour. Shared belief is in turn part of what builds community and cements belonging. Changes in behaviour, especially the change

Christians know as repentance and renewal, are made possible when a sense of belonging, or wanting to belong, makes such change seem desirable and worthwhile. Ultimately, most Christians would say that their faith that through Christ they already belong to God and to each other makes for a distinctive Christian behaviour, a specific take on the complex task of being human.

Belonging is a sociological word, and the word Christians would want to use to describe their particular kind of belonging in all its many senses is Love.

Love as the key

When Jesus was asked to summarize the greatest commandment in the Hebrew Scriptures he quoted a double commandment about love:

> 'You shall love the Lord your God with all your heart and all your soul, and with all your mind . . . and . . . you shall love your neighbour as yourself. On these two commandments hang all the law and the prophets.' (Matthew 22:37–40)

His whole ministry was concerned with rediscovering and renewing these commandments, interpreting in a new way what it means in practice to love God and your neighbour. When he came to pass on his own teaching to his disciples in a memorable way he again used love as his key:

> 'I give you a new commandment, that you love one another. Just as I have loved you, you also should love one another.' (John 13: 34)

For most Christians, however, Jesus is more than just a great teacher and prophet. Christians came to believe, in the years following his death and resurrection, that Jesus was himself a full incarnation and complete manifestation of God. It was from their intimate experience of Jesus as God incarnate that they came to say with confidence not simply that God *gives* or *receives* love but that 'God *is* Love and those who abide in Love abide in God and God abides in them.' (1 John 4:16)

Because it is such a central motif, *love* also provides a key to interpreting many of the Christian doctrines which have sometimes seemed obscure or difficult to those who seek to understand the faith. For example, the theology of *atonement* (see below, p. 61–3), with its many different models and emphases, can be summarized and understood as the restoration of a loving relationship with God, broken by human sinfulness but restored by Christ offering himself to his father. Likewise, the doctrine of God as *Holy Trinity* can best be explained and understood not in terms of abstract personae or states of being and union, but of loving relationships between Father and Son, through the Holy Spirit.

In each section of this book, therefore, as we explore the variety of Christian teaching and practice, everything will be linked back to the central theme of love as a key to understanding what Christians believe.

2

Where are the Christians?

Mapping the message

Like Judaism before it and Islam afterwards, Christianity began in the Middle East. Since then it has spread rapidly, often on the wings of persecution, and is now found throughout the world.

Christianity moved swiftly from its Jewish origins to embrace the idea that its teachings were for all nations. Within a few generations, Christians were to be found throughout the Roman Empire and beyond as far as India. As with other religions, Christianity spread along the routes of trade and conquest opened up both by its adherents and its enemies. After the fall of Jerusalem in AD 70 its centre of gravity moved to Rome and Constantinople, the twin centres of an increasingly divided empire. Ultimately the division between Western Catholic and Eastern Orthodox forms of Christianity reflected this division.

The discovery, exploration, and indeed exploitation by Europeans of the so-called New World in the sixteenth and seventeenth centuries meant that Christian ideas and teaching

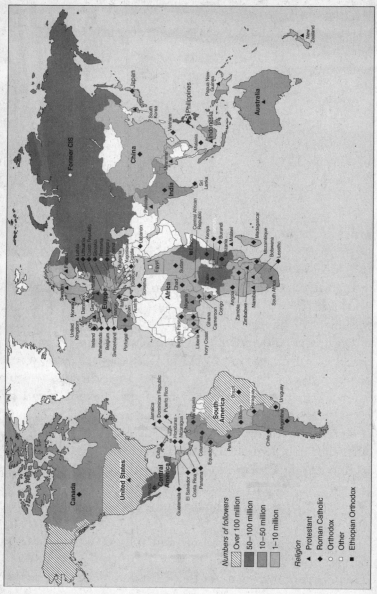

Distribution of the Christian Religion

Numbers of followers
- Over 100 million
- 50–100 million
- 10–50 million
- 1–10 million

Religion
- ▲ Protestant
- ◆ Roman Catholic
- ○ Orthodox
- □ Other
- ■ Ethiopian Orthodox

spread to North and South America. Often it came on the trail of conquerors whose violence and rapacity entirely contradicted the teachings and spirit of Jesus. In spite of this it found roots and flourished so strongly that Christians in the New World soon began to challenge the behaviour of the missionaries and those who backed them. The film *The Mission,* set in the age of the conquistadors, provides a moving study of how a pioneer Christian community in the New World could reveal and challenge the hypocrisy of those very Christians who had founded it. Even today the rise of 'liberation' theology in South America and Africa is forcing the European churches to re-examine the roots of their own beliefs.

This rapid spread through many tribes and languages compelled the Church to make a distinction between Christ and context, to realize that the same inner faith, understood as a 'new life in Christ', could flourish amidst widely different customs and cultures. The first breakthrough came when the Council of Jerusalem (*c.* AD 51), consisting largely of Jewish Christians, gave permission for Gentile Christians not to be circumcised or keep the Jewish law (see Acts Chapter 15). This was a recognition that outward and visible ceremonies might vary while still witnessing to the same inner truth. The same issues are present in the flourishing today of African and Indian Churches, whose liturgy and outlook reflect the best of their own indigenous culture and are not expected to be an imitation of the west.

Indeed a significant factor in the global growth of Christianity is the influence of strong and growing Churches from the developing world on the apparently declining Churches of Europe. In his seminal work *Foolishness to the Greeks: Gospel and Western Culture*, Leslie Newbiggin uses his experience of the culture of Christian Churches in India to criticize the materialism and secularism of nominally Christian Western society. The ceremonies in 2005 for the funeral of Pope John Paul II and the installation of Pope Benedict XVI highlighted the global reach of a Church within which there is both a unity of belief and a great diversity of ethnicity and cultural expression.

Much of Church history is coloured by this tension between unity and diversity. The present disputes within the worldwide Anglican Communion over homosexuality are a case in point. Some see issues in human sexuality as falling within a purely socio-cultural realm where diversity is to be welcomed, where others see them as matters of central belief and teaching which transcend (and indeed bring under judgement) mere human traditions and cultural arrangements. At a recent meeting of bishops from the worldwide Anglican Communion one of the participants remarked: 'We don't need a theologian to help us resolve our differences, we need an anthropologist!'

Christianity came to be divided into three broad streams, Orthodox, Catholic, and Protestant (see below, p. 51–5), and it is still possible to make some generalizations about the distribution of these different branches of the Christian family. It is still, broadly speaking, true that the Orthodox flourish in those places that were once part of the eastern half of the Roman Empire from Greece through into Russia. The continuous Christian presence from earliest times in Palestine, Egypt and other parts of the Near East is also in the Orthodox tradition. It is also, broadly speaking, true that those parts of the world dominated by the Latin- and latterly Spanish-speaking parts of Europe have been and remain part of the Roman Catholic family, whereas the Protestant Reformation took greater hold in northern Europe than in the south. This pattern of European division was then mapped by conquest on to the Americas and later on to Africa and the Far East. So North America is more generally Protestant, South America more generally Catholic. In Colonial Africa the branch of Christianity adhered to by new converts also reflected the Church persuasion of their European political masters. The vast extent of the worldwide Anglican Communion is therefore, in part, a consequence of the power and extent of the British Empire.

These broad-brush generalizations are, however, full of important exceptions and qualifications. Even where the denominational adherence of a post-colonial country is nominally the same as that of its former colonial rulers, the local and lively manifestations of faith are often quite different. Further, the growth of the ecumenical movement (a movement towards unity between denominations through dialogue which had its roots in the Edinburgh missionary conference of 1910) and the spread of global communication mean that there is far more dialogue and exchange between different Christian traditions and cultures than ever before. So for many Christians these old historical lines of demarcation are less and less significant.

Another factor which complicates the traditional picture of the three main branches of Christianity is the emergence of new 'non-denominational' house churches largely among previously 'Protestant' cultures together with the emergence in Catholic cultures of a charismatic movement which has a great deal in common with the 'Protestant' house churches. These churches bear little resemblance to their classic forebears and carry much less of what they would see as the historical baggage of the Reformation and pre-Reformation division. They usually refer to themselves as non-denominational, but emphasize a mixture of biblical literalism and ecstatic experience of release through 'the gifts of the spirit', especially chanting or singing in tongues, a release of sound and syllable which non-believers might regard as random but which believers interpret as the language of angels. Though these 'house churches' began literally in people's houses many of them now occupy disused cinemas and old warehouse buildings in cities across Britain and America. It is not yet clear how far they may eventually harden into full denominations or how far they may presage a movement towards a new unity for all Christians.

Christianity is still a missionary faith and the number of its adherents is still growing. But its centre of gravity is shifting. It is no longer a predominantly western or European faith. Congregations in these historic homelands of Christian faith are declining, while those in Africa, China, India and South America are all on the increase. The Anglican Communion recently declared a decade of evangelism, echoing a similar call by the Roman Catholic Church. That revival, should it succeed, will be driven more by the energy of the young and emerging Churches of the developing world than by the traditions and history of the west.

Even now the range of backgrounds from which some of the best-known theologians and Christian leaders have been drawn is strikingly global and varied. The last Pope emerged from the struggles of Poland; Martin Luther King belonged to the Black American population of the southern states; Mother Theresa came from Albania to minister in Calcutta; Oscar Romero rose to world prominence from his base in San Salvador. In the future, as the balance shifts, we will see more and more Christian leaders and thinkers coming from Africa, from China, and from the Indian subcontinent. As a result we should be able to look forward to a better-informed encounter and dialogue between Christianity and the other world faiths and ideologies. It may even be that this present series of books and others like it will be part of the formation and content of that process.

3

The story of Jesus

History and mystery

One feature of the scripture's style is unique. St Gregory says that *scripture transcends all other sciences by the way it uses one and the same discourse to tell history and reveal mystery* (In *Summa Theologia* by St Thomas Aquinas; a Concise Translation, edited by Timothy McDermott, page four).

How can we come to know anything about Jesus at all? He wrote nothing down, and expected his gospel – the 'good news', as he termed it – about the coming of God's kingdom to be passed by word of mouth from person to person. Moreover, the claim of his immediate followers, and all the subsequent Christian communities, is that these encounters with Jesus did not cease with his death. The core Christian belief, on which all the others is founded, is that Jesus rose from the dead, that he met his followers after his resurrection, and that he promised to be with them, and continue to teach and inspire them till the end of the age.

For members of the Christian faith, there is a twofold

witness to the life and person of Jesus: there are the docu-
mentary records of his earthly life and death, as there might be
with any historical figure, and there is a further strand or tradition of testimony about encounters with Jesus after his
death. These have themselves strongly affected the written
record.

The Christian Bible, with its twenty-seven New Testament
books appended (almost as a commentary) to the existing
books of the Jewish scripture, is woven from both these
strands. It contains accounts of the life and teaching of Jesus
prior to his death and also vivid accounts of people meeting
him afterwards. Most scholars agree that the accounts of Jesus'
life and teaching before his death are informed and illumi-
nated by what has been called the 'Easter experience' – the
encounter with Jesus beyond the Cross and the conviction that
his resurrection was the real key to his identity and to all he did
and said.

What follows is a brief outline of Jesus' life as it is attested in
the gospels. The gospels were themselves based on stories
handed down orally from the earliest witnesses and companions
of Jesus. There is still scholarly debate about the exact dating of
the written gospels, but the consensus is that they came to be
written down between AD 65 and 100, that is, more than 30
years after Jesus' death. While they give us a good idea of what
he did and said, we should also note that they arose in a community of faith and their prime purpose was to express that
community's belief that Jesus was God become human, the
Word made flesh (John 1:14). They are not straightforward
biographies in the modern sense. Many details are recorded
not simply for the sake of their historical or biographical accu-
racy, but because they represent a deeper truth about Jesus. As
Aquinas says at the beginning of his great *Summa* of the

Christian faith, they are there not only to tell history but to reveal mystery.

Sometimes the most important part of a gospel story is not the outward and visible narrative (what you would have seen if you had been there with a camcorder) but the inward and spiritual truth which that story reveals. For example, when we are told that Jesus was born in Bethlehem, the gospel writer intends us to understand this primarily as a statement about Jesus' role as promised Messiah, who, it was prophesied, was to be born there, and his role as the 'bread of life' for all (Bethlehem means literally 'house of bread'), rather than making a merely geographical statement about his origins.

The word *Messiah* means 'anointed' – the Greek word is *Christ*. Anointing with oil signifies that a person has been chosen by God for a special purpose and kings were anointed in the Old Testament as a sign of their office. Both words refer to the widespread expectation amongst Jews, based on Old Testament prophecy, that God would send to them a Messiah, an anointed one, who would save Israel and would also, as some prophecies seemed to imply, be God's sign of salvation to the whole world.

Almost every detail in the gospels has this resonant quality, revealing mystery as well as telling history. It is not meant only as surface detail or biographical background but also as a clue that helps us answer two central questions: Who is this man and what does he reveal of God?

Jesus was born a Jew in Roman-occupied Palestine. The gospels concentrate mainly on the ministry and teaching of his final three years and on his death and resurrection. Two of the four gospels also contain accounts of his birth. That story, so well known and well loved, discloses, in narrative form, some of the deepest mysteries of the Christian faith and has provided

the basis for some of the richest meditations and poetry in suc-
ceeding ages.

The tradition that Jesus was born of a virgin and conceived
of the Holy Spirit (for the Christian understanding of the Holy
Spirit see below, p. 18, 75–7) was first understood as a fulfilment of Old Testament prophecy, proving that he was the
promised Messiah. Later Gentile (non-Jewish) Christians came
to see it as signifying the union in Christ of all things, the
meeting in him of heaven and earth. While understanding its
deeper meanings, most Christians would also accept the
accounts of the virginal conception of Jesus to be literally as
well as symbolically true, a miracle pointing to a mystery.
However, some Western Christians maintain that it is possible
to accept the truth of the mystery without believing literally in
the miracle.

Likewise the stories of how the infant Jesus was visited, recognized and worshipped first by humble Jewish shepherds and
then by three wise men, non-Jews from the East, are intended
to be read by Christian believers as both history and mystery.
The shepherds come to acknowledge him as the 'shepherd' of
Israel, the wise men as the source of all wisdom; the kings
came to him as king of kings. He is shown as the Lord of both
Jew and Gentile. And in the contrast between the kings who
come to worship and Herod the jealous ruler who seeks to
destroy him, the decisive conflict between Jesus (representing
the authority of God) and Pilate and Herod (representing
usurped human ecclesiastical and political authority) is foreshadowed.

The other element in the story of Jesus' birth, which embodies a major theme of his life and ministry and a significant
strand of Christian belief, is the humble and perilous circumstances into which he was born. In the story of his mother's long

journey from Nazareth to Bethlehem, of there being no room at the inn, of his birth in a stable and his cradle a manger, we see the first statement of the persistent Christian teaching that God identifies himself especially with the lowly and the humble. Christians believe that in Christ God expresses his solidarity with humanity at its most wretched and vulnerable. This insight, embodied in the stories of Jesus' birth in a stable and his first years as a homeless refugee on the run from political persecution, was given direct and highly influential theological emphasis in one of the Letters of Saint Paul: 'Though he was in the form of God, he did not regard equality with God as something to be exploited, but emptied himself, taking the form of a slave, being born in human likeness.' (Philippians 2:6–7)

All four of the gospels emphasize the importance of Jesus' baptism in the River Jordan by the prophet John the Baptist. John's baptism of Jesus was a call to the people of Israel to repent and make a completely new start with God, symbolized by a return to the River Jordan. It was the Jordan that the children of Israel had originally crossed into their 'Promised Land', to live out the covenant they had made with God which had been established by Moses. John's message was that their sinfulness had broken this covenant, that they must repent and begin the relationship anew. They must emerge clean from the Jordan as their ancestors had done centuries previously, so that they would be ready for the day (which he believed to be imminent) when God would establish his rule, the Kingdom of Heaven, in their midst through his promised Messiah, the Christ.

This is the setting for the dramatic moment with which the gospels open. The people are coming back to Jordan, as repentant sinners, to await the cataclysmic arrival of the king and his kingdom in the royal city of Jerusalem. But instead the Messiah arrives secretly, presenting himself without ceremony as one of

the multitude of people seeking baptism. In a moment of
revelation John recognizes him and is amazed, saying that he is
not worthy to so much as untie his sandals let alone baptize
him, but Jesus insists that he should be baptized.

What does this signify? Once again, a single outward event
discloses many layers of meaning to Christian believers. Jesus'
baptism and his recognition as the Messiah by John initiated his
public ministry and was followed, after a preparatory period of
fasting and prayer in the wilderness, by his calling of the disciples. It also symbolizes his complete identification and solidarity
with humanity. Although he himself needs no baptism, as John
recognizes, he is nevertheless ritually washed clean of sin on
behalf of Israel, and, as later Christians came to believe, on
behalf of all humanity. Jesus' baptism, as described in the
gospels, also provides the first glimpse, later Christians were to
argue, of his identity as the son within a trinitarian godhead
understood as Father, Son and Holy Spirit. Christians believe
that they can understand God as Father, as Son and as Holy
Spirit – three persons related in a communion of love and still
one God (see below, p. 75–7):

> When He came up out of the water, immediately he saw the
> heavens open and the Spirit descending on him like a dove; and
> a voice came from Heaven, 'Thou art my beloved Son, with
> thee I am well pleased.' (Mark 1:10–11)

Here Christian believers glimpse Father, Son and Holy Spirit
revealed in unique and loving relationship one with another: the
Son coming to the Father through the symbolic waters of baptism, the Father opening heaven to pour his love upon the Son,
and the Holy Spirit descending between them as the essence of
that mutual love.

At the end of the gospels Jesus is portrayed by Matthew as giving his last commandment to his disciples: 'Go therefore and make disciples of all nations, baptizing them in the name of the Father and of the Son and of the Holy Spirit' (Matthew 28:19). In this way the gospel opens, under the figure of baptism, with a revelation of the unique and perfect love between the Son and the Father, and concludes with an invitation to the whole of humanity to enter through Christ into that same loving relationship with God.

John's gospel, which often gives the inner meaning of outer events portrayed in the other three so-called *synoptic* gospels, goes on to say that 'to all who believed in him . . . he gave power to become the children of God' (John 1:12).

Study of the four gospels reveals that there is a large strand of material common to Matthew, Mark and Luke. Viewing them synoptically (alongside one another) scholars have concluded that they must have had a common source, possibly written down, as well as access to different sets of orally transmitted stories. Each gospel writer/compiler has then shaped their material to give a particular emphasis. Matthew has a special emphasis on Jesus' Jewish roots; Luke on his ministry to those on the fringe – outcasts, women and Gentiles; Mark emphasizes the decisive power and immediacy of his miracles and contrasts it with his 'passion' or passive suffering after his arrest. John begins with an assertion of Christ's pre-existent life in God: 'In the beginning was the Word, and the Word was with God, and the Word was God' (John 1:1).

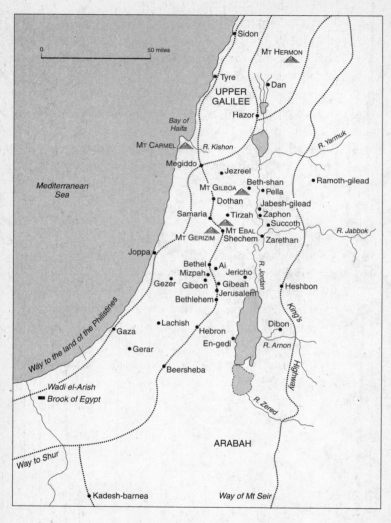

Palestine in the time of Jesus

Between the baptism (which disclosed this unique relationship with the father) and the post-resurrection command that all humanity are invited into that relationship, born again as God's children, lie Jesus' teaching and healing ministry, and above all his death and resurrection. Christians believe that through these events Christ bridged the gap between heaven and earth, restored the broken relationship between God and humanity and made it possible for everyone, like Jesus, to call God 'Our Father'. (The fuller significance of 'The Lord's Prayer' is explored in Chapter 5.)

Jesus' baptism was followed by three years of public ministry: teaching, healing, calling people back to God. During this time he never travelled more than a hundred miles or so from his boyhood home in Nazareth. He began his mission around the shores of Lake Galilee, well away from the centres of religious and political power in Jerusalem and Rome, and then travelled through Samaria and down into the south to Judea, Bethany and Jerusalem itself.

Jerusalem is the setting for the dramatic final week before his crucifixion, when the conflict which had developed between Jesus and the religious authorities of the day was brought to a climax. The substance of his teaching in this period will be dealt with in the next chapter. Here we will look at some of the recorded events which show the context of his teaching and its relevance to the great question posed by the gospels: Who is this man?

The gospels record that immediately after his baptism Jesus 'was led up by the Spirit into the wilderness to be tempted of the devil' (Matthew 4:1).

WHAT DO CHRISTIANS MEAN BY 'THE DEVIL'?

Jesus makes a number of references to a figure variously known as The Devil, Satan, Beelzebub, and 'the prince of this world'. Contemporary Jewish thought believed in the existence of demons – unclean spiritual beings who sought to oppose God's rule. Jesus' authority to cast out these demons was regarded as proof of his claim to be Messiah, God's anointed. In later Christian theology the devil or Satan (the word means 'accuser') was believed to be an angel of God, originally created good, who had 'fallen' from grace in heaven, and sought through deceit to pervert and corrupt mankind, although he and his other 'fallen angels' had been decisively defeated by Jesus on the Cross and could have no final triumph. Contemporary Christians are divided between those who believe that the devil is an objectively existent entity still tempting and prompting the world to evil and those who believe that he is a symbolic personification of the malice which is part of every fallen human being. (We'll come back to original sin below, p. 58–60).

These temptations centred on the question of who Jesus was and what kind of authority, or kingly rule, he was called to exercise. He is tempted to do miracles for his own personal ends, to make a display of miraculous power for self-aggrandizement, and finally to surrender his love and obedience to God in return for unlimited secular power. All these temptations he rejects, making it clear that his understanding of what it is to be Messiah does not involve the claiming of a secular kingdom. However, because Israel was at this time under Roman occupation, there was a strong hope among many of its people that the coming of the true Messiah would signal the violent overthrow of the Roman occupiers and their puppet, King Herod. Many hoped for the establishment of the kingdom of God as a political and national reality on the actual territory of Israel, a perfect and righteous kingdom ruled over in person by the anointed representative of the God of Israel. Given these expectations, anyone claiming to be that Messiah would attract both political and religious attention and would be the object of devotion and hope if those claims proved true and of execration and contempt if they proved false.

Emerging from his period of intense testing and prayer in the wilderness, Jesus seems to have accepted that he was the Messiah but to have arrived at a radical redefinition of the true meaning of that Messianic role. His first action was to build a community. In calling twelve disciples, he was symbolically reconstituting the kingdom of Israel, with its twelve tribes each descended from Israel himself.

Significantly, the twelve people he called to follow him were not selected from a special priestly caste or from racially pure members of each tribe. Rather, they were ordinary folk from the villages of his native Galilee. Peter and James and John were fishermen. Some of the twelve, like Matthew, far from being zealous purists in the anti-Roman cause had even been collaborators with the regime. Also (remarkably for his time and context) Jesus numbered women among his followers, though subsequent patriarchal Christian cultures have questioned whether they should be given the status of disciples or 'apostles' (those who are sent). Amongst these women Mary and her sister Martha and Mary Magdalene are named in the gospels and play a significant role.

The new community Jesus was building was witness to his powerful teaching and also to a series of miracles.

> Jesus went throughout Galilee teaching in their synagogues,
> proclaiming the good news of the kingdom and curing every
> disease and every sickness among the people. So his fame spread
> throughout all Syria and they brought to him all the sick . . .
> and he cured them. And great crowds followed him . . .
> (Matthew 4:23–25)

These miracles were understood to be acts of divine compassion
working through Jesus – signs of who Jesus really was. They
were always accompanied by the proclamation at the heart of
Jesus' mission, the same proclamation which John had made:
'Repent for the Kingdom of Heaven has come near.' That is to
say: stop, turn around, begin again, for the God you felt to be
distant and from whom you were alienated is close by. He is
calling you to become part of his kingdom and to be his people
again. This was the message the true Messiah was expected to
preach, for it was thought that the Messiah himself would inau-
gurate that Kingdom.

Because his miracles were directly linked with his teaching
about the kingdom, they posed very sharply the question of
Jesus' identity as Messiah. They led, early in his ministry, both
to his identification as Messiah by believers and to charges of
blasphemy against him by those who rejected that claim. So, for
example, early on in his ministry Mark records the healing of a
paralytic but is more interested in the inward gift of forgiveness
and restoration than its outward manifestation in physical
healing:

> [3]Then some people came, bringing to him a paralysed man, car-
> ried by four of them. [4]And when they could not bring him to
> Jesus because of the crowd, they removed the roof above him;
> and after having dug through it, they let down the mat on

which the paralytic lay. [5]When Jesus saw their faith, he said to the paralytic, 'Son, your sins are forgiven.' [6]Now some of the scribes were sitting there, questioning in their hearts, [7] 'Why does this fellow speak in this way? It is blasphemy! Who can forgive sins but God alone?' [8]At once Jesus perceived in his spirit that they were discussing these questions among themselves; and he said to them, 'Why do you raise such questions in your hearts? [9]Which is easier, to say to the paralytic, "Your sins are forgiven," or to say, "Stand up and take your mat and walk"? [10]But so that you may know that the Son of Man has authority on earth to forgive sins' [he said to the paralytic] [11]'I say to you, stand up, take your mat and go to your home.' [12]And he stood up, and immediately took the mat and went out before all of them; so that they were all amazed and glorified God, saying, 'We have never seen anything like this!' (Mark 2:3–end New Revised Standard Version)

Who can forgive sins but God? This is the key question. For Jesus' critics this was blasphemy; for his first followers it was a sign that he might be the Messiah, God's human emissary, to whom such an authority to forgive would have been delegated. For later Christians who believed that Jesus was not only the promised Messiah of God but also God himself incarnate, the question 'Who can forgive sins but God?' had a clear answer: Nobody but God himself can forgive sins, and it is indeed God himself, in Jesus, in our midst, who is doing just that. As Saint Paul was later to say, 'In Christ God was reconciling the world to himself.' (2 Corinthians 5:19)

Likewise, the various 'nature miracles' which are recorded in the gospels (Jesus' stilling of the storm, walking on water, multiplying loaves and fishes and turning water into wine) all have this many-layered quality. They link Jesus with Old Testament prophecy and the expectation of the Messiah, but also ascribe to him a creative power and command over nature which could only be attributed to God himself. Again and again his miracles provoke the question: Who is this?

Some modern commentators tend to 'rationalize' or 'demythologize' the gospel narrative, so as to make it fit in with western scientific materialism. They see these miracles primarily as pictorial symbols of Jesus' identity, allegorical episodes that did not necessarily happen in the way they are described. But many Christians regard the miracles as having been historical as well as symbolic events and their historicity is seen as a sign of God's active involvement in the midst of his creation.

Gradually Jesus' followers came to believe that he was indeed the Messiah, the anointed and chosen one. But at the same time they were being taught by Jesus that the 'good news' of his kingdom was more radical and far-reaching than they had imagined. It could not be contained in the small expectations of a temporary kingship in just one kingdom of the earth, or in the overthrow of just one political system. The establishment of God's kingdom would be stranger and more far-reaching than any mere nationalist uprising against the Romans. But because the contemporary expectation that the Messiah would lead a nationalist revolt was so strong, there was a real danger of mis-understanding if Jesus were to be identified as the Messiah in the popular sense of that term before he had demonstrated the true nature of that office. For this reason he is often recorded as asking those he has healed not to tell anyone (e.g. Matthew 8:3–5).

For Jesus, the miracles were both acts of compassion and ways of teaching about who he was and what it really meant for him to be Messiah. It sometimes took his followers many years of subsequent prayer and experience to apprehend their meaning. This discovery of meaning is then woven into the way the stories were passed on in the oral tradition and eventually written down. An example of a pair of related miracles whose true significance could not have been seen at the time can be found in the turning of water into wine and the feeding of the five thousand. Both of these miracles are described as having taken place early in Jesus' ministry, but their deeper significance only became apparent after the Last Supper, when Jesus identified his blood with the wine and his body with the bread. Jesus spoke at this meal of a new covenant, which is re-enacted during Holy Communion – a central and defining rite of the new Church. (See Chapter 6: What do Christians do?)

All the gospels attest that Jesus found himself in conflict with the authorities from early on in his public ministry, a struggle which, in Matthew's gospel, is foreshadowed by the story that even in Jesus' infancy King Herod had tried to kill him. At the heart of the conflict was the question of authority. Time and again the gospels attest that Jesus taught and acted 'as one with authority' (Matthew 7:29, Mark 1:22). Those who had placed themselves in positions of power and were seeking to bolster their position wanted to know 'by whose authority' Jesus was teaching.

An early focus for this conflict was Jesus' interpretation of the Torah, the Law of Moses. Jesus honoured the Torah and said he had come to fulfil it, but he also interpreted it in a way that was a challenge to the strict legalism of emergent groups like the Pharisees. The Pharisees represented a distinct school of thought within Judaism with a special emphasis on the keeping of the Law in Torah as strictly and exactly as possible. They were a national organization with a large number of local groups, capable of exerting real political pressure. There were as many as 6,000 actively organized Pharisees in the time of Jesus. Saint

Paul, before his conversion to Christianity, had been a Pharisee. We have already seen how Jesus made his healing of the paralytic a sign that 'the son of Man has Authority on earth to forgive sins' (Mark 2:10). Almost immediately afterwards the same gospel records conflict about Sabbath keeping. The Pharisees were very strict about keeping the Sabbath as a complete day of rest on which no work of any kind could be undertaken, whereas for Jesus the principle of love and compassion was to be the guide for all interpretation of any religious code or Law. He makes this clear by healing a man on the Sabbath:

> Again he entered the synagogue and a man was there who had a withered hand. They watched him to see whether he would cure him on the Sabbath, so that they might accuse him. And he said to the man who had the withered hand: 'Come forward.' Then he said to them: 'Is it Lawful to do good or to do harm on the Sabbath, to save life or to kill?' And they were silent. He looked around at them with anger. He was grieved at their hardness of heart and said to the man: 'Stretch out your hand.' He stretched it out and his hand was restored. The Pharisees went out and immediately conspired with the Herodians how to destroy him. (Mark 2:23–3:6)

These are themes which characterized not only the rest of Jesus' ministry but also the whole subsequent history of Christianity. Jesus confronts his own religious tradition which, like the hand of the man, has become withered and lifeless. At the heart of the Law and the traditions, including the establishment of the Sabbath, he sees God's compassion for humanity and his commandment of Love. This, he asserts, constitutes the true life of religion, without which it withers

into arrogant legalism and power play. In breaking the Sabbath
to heal the withered arm he was seeking to restore the original
purpose of a withered Law. He is constantly challenging the
outer to restore the inner, breaking the letter of the Law to
restore its spirit. In the present debates amongst Christian
believers about the ordination of women and attitudes to
homosexuality, and in earlier debates about slavery, the same
issues are at stake. Throughout its history the letter of the
Church's laws and traditions has been challenged in the name
and spirit of its founder.

The plots to destroy Jesus, referred to so early in Mark's
gospel, come to a head in his final visit to Jerusalem and particularly during the events of the last week of his life. These are
attested in all four gospels, enshrined in subsequent Christian
liturgy (that is to say the forms of worship used by the Church),
and are remembered throughout the keeping of Holy Week to
this day.

The key event at the beginning of the confrontation in
Jerusalem leading to Jesus' arrest and execution is his 'triumphal'
entry into Jerusalem, riding on a donkey accompanied by a
crowd hailing him as 'the son of David' and 'he who comes in
the name of the Lord'. This was both a defiant public accept-
ance of the role of Messiah and also a nuanced reading of it.
Had he entered on a warhorse it might have been a signal for
rebellion. In choosing a donkey he chose to recall and fulfil an
earlier prophecy, in the books of Isaiah and Zechariah, that the
true King would come to his people in meekness.

Having entered Jerusalem, Jesus went to the temple, the
centre of the religious power, to carry out the symbolic act
which later Christians referred to as 'the cleansing of the
temple'.

Then Jesus entered the temple and drove out all who were sell-
ing and buying in the temple, and he overturned the tables of
the moneychangers and the seats of those who sold doves. [13]He
said to them, 'It is written, "My house shall be called a house of
prayer"; but you are making it a den of robbers.' (Matthew
21:12–13)

In theory the moneychangers' role was to protect the sanctity of
the temple by assuring that no unclean pagan money defiled it,
but this over-scrupulous keeping of purity law formed an economic as well as psychological barrier between God and his
people. In demolishing this barrier Jesus was expressing in symbolic terms the restoration of free access to the heart of God.
Such an action also made it virtually certain that those whose
authority he so openly challenged would seek to destroy him.

From this moment on, the gospel narratives are filled with a
sense of the coming end but also, beyond it, with the hints and
promises of resurrection. It is in this context that Jesus' most
powerful and moving teaching on love, service and self-sacrifice
was given to his disciples. Some of the teaching came as public
declamation in the temple, in his challenges to the authorities,
and some was disclosed in the intimate setting of his 'last
supper' with the disciples. This key event, on the Thursday of
that week, the night of his betrayal and arrest, is understood by
Christians to be the foundation of their central, formative
ritual, the Holy Communion. Communion has a different
emphasis in different branches of Christianity (see below,
p. 79–80) but all Christians agree that it is fundamental to the
understanding and recollection of their faith.

As with everything else in the gospels the Last Supper is an
event which resonates on many levels. It is both history and
mystery. Jesus and his disciples had come to Jerusalem to keep

the feast of the Passover. The gospels differ as to whether the Last Supper was itself the Passover meal, but it is significant that the great memorial meal of Christianity, which symbolizes and enacts a new covenant between God and humanity, was founded in the context of the Passover meal which recalled the Old Testament Covenant between God and Israel.

The significance of this supper for subsequent generations of Christians is discussed later in this book. It is clear, however, that in referring to the broken bread as his body and the wine outpoured as his blood Jesus was not only prophesying his violent death, but suggesting that his death would have a purpose and meaning. That meaning, like the ritual meal itself, would include forgiveness and restoration of love between God and humanity and between God's people. In referring to the wine as 'my blood of the covenant which is poured out for many for the forgiveness of sins' (Matthew 26:28) Jesus may have been interpreting his coming death by associating himself with the lambs sacrificed at Passover. This sacrifice recalled the story told in the book of Exodus that it was the blood of a lamb, painted as a sign on their doorways, which allowed the children of Israel to be 'passed over' and saved from the angel of death in Egypt. This is also why John the Baptist is shown pointing to Jesus as 'the Lamb of God'. It is crucial for an understanding of what happened immediately after this meal – the betrayal, arrest, trial and crucifixion of Jesus – because it interprets those events as being within God's will, and therefore as validating his claim to be the Messiah.

For all the differences between Jesus' disciples (who believed his claim to be Messiah) and the religious authorities (who rejected that claim), they were all orthodox Jews who believed that God was at work in the very fabric of history, in and through what happened to his people. At the heart of the arrest and trial of Jesus was the idea that the truth of his claim to be God's special emissary or agent, or to be identified in some more intimate and mysterious way with God himself, would be tested by events. If he *was* God's son or Messiah then God would vindicate him. God would not permit the Messiah to be falsely charged and executed by the very priesthood whose job it was to prepare the world for his arrival. He would intervene or give a sign. This is the logic of Jesus' trial right down to the final calls to him: 'If you are the Son of God, come down from the Cross.'

Jesus' prosecutors were working on the assumption that the Messiah would be a powerful character, not a weak one. The fact that he had been arrested and was meekly undergoing torment in silence at their hands already counted against him, and his ignominious crucifixion in public in a ritually outcast and unclean place clinched the case. Had he been who he claimed, God would have rescued and vindicated him. That even some of his disciples were inclined to read events in this way is made clear by the story of the road to Emmaus (see below, p. 39–40).

Had the story ended with Jesus' ignominious death, his disciples would have been obliged eventually to accept that they had been deluded by a false Messiah. Everything therefore turns on the resurrection. It is in the light of the belief that God absolutely and unequivocally vindicated Christ's claim by raising him from the dead that all the Christian documents about his life have been written. If God raised him from the dead, then the death itself must have had meaning. Instead of signifying God's rejection of Jesus, as the scribes and Pharisees thought, Christians came to believe that the crucifixion of Jesus was at the heart of God's plans and purpose for humanity.

In the light of the resurrection, the crucifixion was seen as God's way of identifying with humanity in the midst of rejection and alienation, of his solidarity with all who are, as Jesus was, under judgement. Christians began to see the Cross as the way through and beyond judgement, as the key to forgiveness and restored love. The gospels therefore especially record and emphasize the sayings of Jesus which anticipate this understanding, which show that he himself saw the Cross as coming within his father's loving purposes for the world. So Mark attests that Jesus, before he and the disciples took the road to Jerusalem, said:

'For the son of Man came not to be served but to serve and to give his life as a ransom for many.' (Mark 10:45)

John records Jesus as saying, quite early in his ministry in one of the most frequently quoted passages in Christian Scripture:

'For God so loved the world that he gave his only Son, so that everyone who believes in him may not perish but may have eternal life.' (John 3:16)

Christians read the gospel accounts therefore as the narrative of events which to all the world looked like an unmitigated disaster, but which to the believing community marked the beginning of a new covenant between God and humanity. Jesus' condemnation, agony and death were understood as a turning point of history. These were the events in and through which a lost and condemned humanity was found, forgiven, and restored into a loving relationship with God. All this is in some sense prefigured in the Last Supper, the covenant meal, which took on vital new significance in the light of Jesus' subsequent death and resurrection.

After the Last Supper, Jesus led his followers to a garden in

Gethsemane where he entered into a period of intense prayer during which he faced the darkness and terror of the death by torture which lay ahead of him. Jesus is described as opening to God his natural human desire to avoid it, but concluding his prayer, 'Nevertheless not my will but thy will be done.' Christians came to believe that in surrendering himself so completely to the will of his father he was offering perfect obedience to God on behalf of all humanity as part of his mission to reconcile the world to God in Love. (See the discussion of atonement below, p. 60–3.)

After this period of prayer, the gospel narratives go on to describe the arrest, trial and execution of Jesus. His various trials – before Caiaphas representing priestly religious authority, before Herod representing the puppet Judaic state, and before Pilate representing the governing Roman authority, which alone could authorize the death penalty – all turn on the question of who Jesus is or claims to be. Matthew's account makes clear the issue at stake:

> Then the high priest said to him, 'I put you under oath before the living God. Tell us if you are the Messiah, the Son of God.' Jesus said to him, 'You have said so. But I tell you from now on you will see the Son of Man seated at the right hand of power and coming on the clouds of heaven.' Then the high priest tore his clothes and said, 'He has blasphemed. Why do we still need witnesses?' (Matthew 26:62–65)

Jesus was then sent to Pontius Pilate, the Roman governor, for sentencing. The gospel accounts make it clear that Pilate was uncomfortable about the case, but agreed to have Jesus executed as a matter of political expediency, for fear that leniency would be interpreted by his masters as a failure to deal with insurrection (John 19:12). Having had Jesus flogged, Pilate ordered that he should be crucified, a form of execution designed to inspire fear and loathing in the Jewish population who believed that to die suspended between earth and heaven was to be particularly accursed.

The site of execution, Golgotha, 'the place of the skull', was chosen because it was the rubbish tip of Jerusalem and therefore, to a society whose central religious observance involved strict cleanliness and purity, a place of complete execration. The religious rulers saw this place as a fitting end to Jesus' blasphemous pretensions to be God's chosen son and Messiah. Christian believers came to see it as the ultimate sign of God's self-emptying love in rescuing humankind – that he would follow humanity into the worst cesspits of corruption, share the worst and most accursed of sufferings, find and forgive us even there. It is therefore a matter both of the history and the mystery of Christian faith that Jesus was crucified alongside two other condemned criminals, and that words of forgiveness were on his lips as the nails were driven in.

> They crucified Jesus there with the criminals, one on his right and one on his left. Then Jesus said 'Father forgive them for they do not know what they are doing.' (Luke 23:33–34)

Just as the last week of his life had begun with his throwing down of a barrier in the outer court of the temple so now the moment of his death was linked back to a symbolic event in the temple:

> Then Jesus gave a loud cry and breathed his last. And the curtain of the temple was torn in two from top to bottom. (Mark 15:37–38)

This curtain or veil was set up between the inner court and the *sanctus sanctorum*, the holy of holies, an inner recess which contained the Ark of the Covenant. This was the sacred chest in which it was believed the copy of the Law given directly to Moses by God was stored, so it represented symbolically the very dwelling place of God. The inner sanctuary was curtained off and could only be entered once a year on the Day of Atonement by the high priest. He entered through the veil bearing the blood of a sacrifice on his body and carrying, sewn into his garment, the names of all the tribes of Israel.

By telling us that this veil was torn in two at the moment of Christ's death, the gospel writers were identifying him as a true high priest. They were suggesting that his death, far from being the seal of God's cursing and rejection of Jesus, was in fact the fulfilment of all the old temple rituals, not in the shadowy forms of symbol but in the living flesh of Jesus. His death had done away with the veil that hung between God and humanity and in his person he was taking the lost world for which he had died back to the heart of the Father.

All four gospels are full of circumstantial detail about how Jesus was taken down from the Cross and buried. This is because they are aware that the claims they make for him rest on the truth of their assertion that God raised him from the dead.

Having been pierced through the heart to make sure he was dead, Jesus was taken down from the Cross and buried in a rock-hewn tomb whose entrance was sealed with a large stone. Normally there would have been a time before such burial when mourners would anoint and prepare the body for burial. This could not be done immediately because he died on the eve of the Sabbath, on which no work could be done.

The gospels recount that early on the first day of the week

(the day that would become Sunday for subsequent generations of Christians) three women from among his disciples
went to the rock tomb in order to anoint his body, as should
have been done before his burial:

> 'They had been saying to one another, "Who will roll the stone
> away for us from the entrance to the tomb?" When they looked
> up they saw that the stone, which was very large, had already
> been rolled back.' (Mark 16:3–4)

They discovered the tomb was empty and had a vision of angels
who told them:

> 'Do not be alarmed; you are looking for Jesus of Nazareth, who
> was crucified. He has been raised. He is not here. Look, there is
> the place where they laid him.'(Mark 16:6)

The different gospels recount a series of encounters between the
disciples and the risen Jesus. Sometimes he appears to them
individually, as he did to Mary Magdalene, sometimes to a
group of them together. He appears to them in the midst of a
locked room, but he also insists on the physicality of his risen
body, inviting Thomas, who had doubted his resurrection, to
touch his wounds. On more than one occasion he shares a meal
with the disciples. The gospels make it clear that they are not
encounters with a ghost. The gospel writers believe Jesus rose
bodily and his tomb was empty. Nevertheless, they also make it
clear that his risen body was in some sense 'glorified', not subject to the same restrictions as their own mortal bodies.

Stories of encounters with the risen Jesus are not confined to
the four gospels. One of the most significant of all was the
encounter between Jesus and Paul, a zealous Pharisee who up to

that moment believed Jesus to have been a blasphemer who had
got his just deserts. This episode on the road to Damascus
changed Paul's life and determined the future course of
Christian history (see below, p. 44–8). Paul himself mentions it
last of all in a list of resurrection appearances recorded in a
letter probably written before any of the gospel accounts of the
resurrection were compiled and containing what scholars
believe to be the earliest Christian creed:

> For I handed on to you as of first importance what I in turn had
> received: that Christ died for our sins in accordance with the
> scriptures, [4]and that he was buried, and that he was raised on
> the third day in accordance with the scriptures, [5]and that he
> appeared to Cephas, then to the twelve. [6]Then he appeared to
> more than five hundred brothers and sisters at one time, most
> of whom are still alive, though some have died.[d] [7]Then he
> appeared to James, then to all the apostles. [8]Last of all, as to one
> untimely born, he appeared also to me. [9]For I am the least of
> the apostles, unfit to be called an apostle, because I persecuted
> the Church of God. (1Corinthians 15:3–9)

However different they were in form, all these encounters had
a similar effect: the doubts, despondency or grief of disciples
like Thomas, Peter and Mary Magdalene were met and
addressed by Jesus, who restored their sense of purpose and
sent them out into the world to continue his work, announcing
the reconciliation of God and humanity. These encounters also
embody a deep paradox, with which the Church has lived ever
since, about the nature of Jesus' continued presence after the
resurrection. On the one hand he promises to be with his disciples always:

'And remember I am with you always, to the end of the age.'
(Matthew 28:20) (These are the closing words of Matthew's
gospel.)

On the other hand he speaks of going away, of ascending to his
father, an ascension which is described at the end of Luke's
gospel and again at the beginning of the Acts of the Apostles:

> Then he led them out as far as Bethany, and, lifting up his
> hands, he blessed them. [51]While he was blessing them, he with-
> drew from them and was carried up into heaven. [52]And they
> worshipped him, and returned to Jerusalem with great joy;
> [53]and they were continually in the temple blessing God. (Luke
> 24:50–end)

In John's gospel Jesus speaks of going to prepare a place for his
disciples, so that where he is, they may be too. It seems that
these early believers had an experience of the risen Jesus in
which they were aware of his being both present with them in
their struggles in this world *and also* with his Father in heaven.
The sense of his presence with the believer was increasingly
focused on a shared meal amongst his followers, the broken
bread and wine outpoured, but he could also be known and
served in and through other people. His earthly body was now
both broken bread and a living community. The sense of his
presence with and to the Father in heaven was expressed in the
universal practice of ending prayers to the Father with the words
'through Jesus Christ our Lord'.

These insights, which were to be developed in the course of
Christian history, are already foreshadowed in two powerful
gospel stories.

In the story of the road to Emmaus a stranger joins two

disciples on their journey, still in the first shock of grief and horror after the crucifixion. He asks them about their troubles. They explain how Jesus, who they had hoped was Messiah, had not been crowned with glory in Jerusalem but had instead been crucified. But now they have heard rumours of his resurrection and don't know what to make of it. The stranger gives them new hope by showing them how the scriptures had prophesied the Messiah's death and resurrection. They press him to stay with them and share a meal, and as he takes bread, blesses and breaks it, they recognize that it is in fact Jesus who is in their midst.

This combination of hospitality to the stranger and the blessed and broken bread as the key to knowing Jesus' presence also echoes the account he himself gives, in Matthew's gospel, about how he can be known and encountered between now and the end of the age. Describing a final judgement, he asks his disciples to imagine him as king at the end of the age, thanking people for having helped and served him:

35'For I was hungry and you gave me food, I was thirsty and you gave me something to drink, I was a stranger and you welcomed me, 36I was naked and you gave me clothing, I was sick and you took care of me, I was in prison and you visited me.' 37Then the righteous will answer him, 'Lord, when was it that we saw you hungry and gave you food, or thirsty and gave you something to drink? 38And when was it that we saw you a stranger and welcomed you, or naked and gave you clothing? 39And when was it that we saw you sick or in prison and visited you?' 40And the king will answer them, 'Truly I tell you, just as you did it to one of the least of these who are members of my family, you did it to me.' (Matthew 25:35–40)

Here Jesus shows that after his resurrection he is as much to be encountered hidden in the lives of the poor whom he loved as in the sacraments and memorials of the Church founded in his name.

Who did Jesus claim to be?

There can be no purely factual account of an 'historical Jesus' though many attempts have been made, particularly in the nineteenth century, to compose a single supposedly objective narrative. The truth is that every story told about Jesus, whether in the first gospels or in later 'reconstructions', always involves interpretation and always comes back to the question of his real identity. In this final section, before we turn to the story of his followers, it is worth looking at who Jesus himself claimed to be according to those gospels.

The key moment in the gospel narratives comes with Peter's recognition of Jesus as Messiah, as they made their last journey to Jerusalem:

> Now when Jesus came into the district of Caesarea Philippi, he asked his disciples, 'Who do people say that the Son of Man is?' [14]And they said, 'Some say John the Baptist, but others Elijah, and still others Jeremiah or one of the prophets.' [15]He said to them, 'But who do you say that I am?' [16]Simon Peter answered, 'You are the Messiah, the Son of the living God.' [17]And Jesus answered him, 'Blessed are you, Simon son of Jonah! For flesh and blood has not revealed this to you, but my Father in heaven.' (Matthew 16:13–17)

So Jesus affirmed himself to be the long-awaited Messiah of Judaism, but did his claims go any further? As we shall see, the most significant development of the early Church was the fact that within a generation it had broken out from a purely Jewish conclave and begun to proclaim a message of salvation for all the world, for Gentiles as much as for Jews. The gospels record a number of episodes in which Jesus locates his ministry outside the chosen people, ministering to Samaritans and Gentiles, finding praiseworthy faith even in a centurion in the occupying Roman army. The most significant claims for an identity and purpose that go beyond the religion and culture into which he was born are to be found in a series of sayings ascribed to Jesus in John's gospel and known collectively as the 'I am' sayings. Some scholars believe that these sayings of Jesus in John's gospel represent a later development of belief about Jesus that has been written back into the narrative life, but others believe that John preserves original material which was not available to the compilers of the synoptic gospels. In either case the existence of the 'I am' sayings shows that some of the earliest witnesses to Jesus' life and teachings believed that he was *one with God* and was speaking to them directly with divine authority.

The 'I am' sayings have a special significance because 'I am' (*ego eimi* in the Greek text of the gospel) equates, in the way Jesus used it, to 'I am who I am', the name of God, transliterated *Yahweh* in the Torah. When Jesus used this formula, his contemporaries understood that he was identifying himself with God, hence the accusation of blasphemy by those who disbelieved his claim. (The gospel is written in Greek, though Jesus himself would have spoken in Aramaic. It is possible though that the formality of the Greek is reflecting Jesus' use of direct quotation from the Hebrew scriptures, which would certainly have been deemed blasphemous.)

⁵⁶'Your ancestor Abraham rejoiced that he would see my day; he saw it and was glad.' ⁵⁷Then the Jews said to him, 'You are not yet fifty years old, and have you seen Abraham?' ⁵⁸Jesus said to them, 'Very truly, I tell you, *before Abraham was, I am.*' ⁵⁹So they picked up stones to throw at him, but Jesus hid himself and went out of the temple. (John 8:56–59)

The 'I am' sayings identify Jesus with the God of Abraham, with God understood as king of the Universe, as the God of the cosmos who is the source of all being and will be the fulfilment of the deepest needs of all people. So in the 'I am' sayings Jesus is seen as identifying himself with the most profound and universal elements of life as symbols of the divine. This chapter has asked the question 'Who is Jesus?' In John's gospel Jesus replies:

I am the bread of life . . .
I am the true vine . . .
I am the door . . .
I am the good shepherd . . .
I am the way, the truth and the life . . .

4

The followers of Jesus

Saint Paul

After Jesus, the most significant figure in the story of
Christianity is Saint Paul. His encounter with the risen Christ
on the road to Damascus is the turning point in the story of
how Christianity moved from being a sect within Judaism to
becoming a world religion.

It is not known when Paul was born, but he was martyred
between AD 62 and 65, and was converted around AD 33. He is,
in other words, a contemporary of Jesus. His teaching is to be
found in a collection of letters which have become part of the
New Testament Christian scriptures. The key letters, containing
the kernel of his doctrine, were all written between AD 50 and
65, before any of the gospels, making them the earliest
Christian documents we have.

The story of Paul's conversion is told by Luke in Acts and by
Paul himself in several of his letters. Assuming, on the evidence
of his crucifixion, that Christ's claims had been false, Paul, then
named Saul, was involved in trying to stamp out the new

'followers of the Way' as Christians then called themselves. St Luke takes up the story:

> Meanwhile Saul, still breathing threats and murder against the disciples of the Lord, went to the high priest [2] and asked him for letters to the synagogues at Damascus, so that if he found any who belonged to the Way, men or women, he might bring them bound to Jerusalem. [3] Now as he was going along and approaching Damascus, suddenly a light from heaven flashed around him. [4] He fell to the ground and heard a voice saying to him, 'Saul, Saul, why do you persecute me?' [5] He asked, 'Who are you, Lord?' The reply came, 'I am Jesus, whom you are persecuting. [6] But get up and enter the city, and you will be told what you are to do.' [7] The men who were travelling with him stood speechless because they heard the voice but saw no one. [8] Saul got up from the ground, and though his eyes were open, he could see nothing; so they led him by the hand and brought him into Damascus. (Acts 9:1–8)

It is highly significant that the voice says to him not 'Why are you persecuting *my followers*?' but 'Why are you persecuting *me*?' The realization that the risen Christ was somehow *in* his followers and they *in* him became a cornerstone of Paul's teaching and theology. A second theme, which also has its roots in this conversion experience, is Paul's teaching that salvation is a gift from God. Our salvation, according to Paul, arises from God's initiative, his loving approach to find us while we are still helpless, a loving initiative which Paul calls grace.

After his conversion Paul became the great missionary and theologian of the early Church, the one who grasped that the gospel was for the entire world, not just for the Jews. This led to controversy as the first Jewish Christians, following their original religion, assumed that any new convert from the Gentile world would have to become Jewish first. They should be circumcised, come within the covenant, and keep the law before accepting Jesus as Messiah.

Paul's great insight was that the coming of Christ was a new beginning for everyone, Jew and Gentile alike, and had nothing to do with outer observance or circumcision, but was about entering with Christ, through faith, into his death and resurrection to be included with him in the loving embrace of the Father. Furthermore, Paul realized that human religious systems, with their laws and hierarchies, gradations and human distinctions, might be a hindrance rather than a help. He taught that religion itself could become a manifestation of sinful pride, standing between God and humanity. Paul concluded that all people had 'sinned' and fallen short of the glory of God, whatever their race or culture and however advanced their religious life, but that God shows love and mercy to everyone, high and low alike, without regard to any human distinction. This radical teaching has been rediscovered time and again in Christian history, especially at times when the Church has accumulated to itself the trappings of formal religion and forgotten the radical mercy of God.

But the deepest root of all Paul's teaching was the same as the root of Christ's teaching: the doctrine of Love, the belief that God's love finds us in Christ and releases in us a powerful responding love for God and for all his creatures. In his first letter to the Church in Corinth Paul wrote a description of Love.

If I speak in the tongues of mortals and of angels, but do not have love, I am a noisy gong or a clanging cymbal. [2]And if I have prophetic powers, and understand all mysteries and all knowledge, and if I have all faith, so as to remove mountains, but do not have love, I am nothing. [3]If I give away all my possessions, and if I hand over my body so that I may boast,[a] but do not have love, I gain nothing.

[4] Love is patient; love is kind; love is not envious or boastful or arrogant [5]or rude. It does not insist on its own way; it is not irritable or resentful; [6]it does not rejoice in wrongdoing, but rejoices in the truth. [7]It bears all things, believes all things, hopes all things, endures all things.

[8] Love never ends. But as for prophecies, they will come to an end; as for tongues, they will cease; as for knowledge, it will come to an end. [9]For we know only in part, and we prophesy only in part; [10]but when the complete comes, the partial will come to an end. [11]When I was a child, I spoke like a child, I thought like a child, I reasoned like a child; when I became an adult, I put an end to childish ways. [12]For now we see in a mirror, dimly,[b] but then we will see face to face. Now I know only in part; then I will know fully, even as I have been fully known. [13]And now faith, hope, and love abide, these three; and the greatest of these is love. (I Corinthians 13)

This is among the most famous and widely quoted of all the Christian scriptures. A prayer for the new Christians in Ephesus, attributed to Paul, sums up his understanding of what it means to be Christian:

For this reason I bow my knees before the Father, [15]from whom every family in heaven and on earth takes its name. [16]I pray that, according to the riches of his glory, he may grant that you may be strengthened in your inner being with power through his Spirit, [17]and that Christ may dwell in your hearts through faith, as you are being rooted and grounded in love. [18]I pray that you may have the power to comprehend, with all the saints, what is the breadth and length and height and depth, [19]and to know the love of Christ that surpasses knowledge, so that you may be filled with all the fullness of God. (Ephesians 3:14–19)

Paul's is a complicated legacy, and he has been appealed to equally as a root-and-branch reformer and a conservative patriarch.

The witnesses of Christ's resurrection, including Paul, became known as 'Apostles', meaning 'those who are sent'. They went out into the world to tell the story of Jesus and proclaim the gospel of how God had come to meet humanity, to find and save them. The story of how they first fared in the world is told from a Christian point of view in the Acts of the Apostles. Acts recounts an event called Pentecost, a Jewish feast day during which the small group of apostles experienced what they believed to be the immediate presence of God as Holy Spirit. Acts tells how this experience confirmed their faith in Jesus and gave them gifts of language and interpretation, which enabled them to share their gospel powerfully with all they met.

The emperor Constantine

Pentecost marks the beginning of the Church's worldwide mission. Christianity spread rapidly, especially amongst the poor and marginalized in the vast Roman Empire. By AD 200 it had spread throughout that Empire and into Mesopotamia. As we have seen, there was already debate in the early Church about how Christians should relate to the nation and culture in which they found themselves. How should they express their distinctive allegiance to Christ and the kingdom of God while remaining engaged with the world Christ had loved and died for?

This debate was sharpened by the enormous challenge and opportunity offered the Church by the conversion of the emperor Constantine (c.272–337). The first 'Christian' emperor, Constantine exercised an enormous though not entirely benign influence on the Church. Tradition has it that before the battle of Milvian Bridge just north of Rome (a battle he was fighting against a rival emperor, Maxentius, in order to consolidate personal power as Roman emperor), Constantine saw a vision of the Cross in the sky and an angel said '*In hoc signo vincit*' ('Conquer through this sign'). Had the same message come to a man like Martin Luther King he might have understood it to mean, 'Only conquer through the Cross and not the sword, through the way of suffering love, not the way of violent coercion'. As it was, Constantine removed the imperial eagle from his Roman standards and weaponry, replaced it with the Kai-Ro (two Greek letters signifying 'Christ', and proceeded to the slaughter. Though he won his Imperial battle, some Christians would argue that the real battle, the battle to preserve the radical teaching of Jesus that we should love our enemy, was lost that night.

Constantine is the first in a line of rulers and politicians who have tried with varying degrees of success to balance the teachings of faith with the exigencies of *realpolitik*. All subsequent Christian debate about relations between Church and state

refers back in one way or another to changes made and issues
raised during his reign.

On the one hand some Christian teachings can be seen to
have had an influence on the way the emperor shaped policy
and law:

> His policy and legislation, though not free from grave blem-
> ishes, show a strongly Christian tendency from the first. He
> humanized the criminal law and the law of debt, mitigated the
> conditions of slavery, made grants to support poor children,
> thus discouraging the exposure of unwanted babies . . . (*The
> Oxford Dictionary of the Christian Church*, 3rd edition, edited by
> EA Livingstone, OUP 1997, page 405)

On the other hand the power politics and militarism of empire
were imported directly into the Church and have exercised a
malign influence ever since. In one of the great ironies of history
the Church whose founder had been persecuted as a heretic by
religious authorities was setting up its own persecuting authorities, and using the very same machinery of the same state that
had executed its founder.

> Within two generations a persecuted Church had become not
> merely an established Church, but a Church with all the power
> of the state at her disposal for the persecution of heretics and the
> compulsory baptism of pagans. The power was excessive and so
> was the price that had to be paid for it . . . (Culture and Mission
> HF Guite Theological Bulletin Vol. III no. 6 May 1975)

The establishment of Christianity as an official religion of
empire not only influenced (some would say compromised)
theology, it also had far-reaching effects on the development of

Church and society. Towards the end of the third century AD the Roman Empire had been divided into an eastern and a western section. Constantine established a second Imperial city in the east, Constantinople (later Byzantium, now Istanbul). After the fall of Rome to the Goths in 410 the two imperial centres developed separately as did the Churches, increasingly divided by language and culture. In the west religious authority was centralized and focused in the hands of the bishop of Rome, who became known as the pope. In the wake of Constantine the bishops of Rome also came to exercise considerable secular power and influence and to claim authority, in the name of Christ 'the king of kings', over emperors and monarchs. In the east the patriarch of Constantinople was head of the Church. Power and ecclesiastical authority were more diffuse and locally centred than in the west, though the Church continued to depend for its well-being on its relations with the various contenders for the imperial throne.

Given their comparatively separate development, doctrinal divisions grew up between east and west. Finally, in a tragic schism in 1054 which has yet to be healed, the leaders of the two Churches formally excommunicated one another. Their unresolved differences concerned the way the role of God the Holy Spirit within the Holy Trinity is defined, and the Papal claim to authority over the whole Church, east as well as west. These questions of authority, and of conflicting claims to doctrinal purity, have exercised the Church ever since.

Constantine, while giving Christianity official status, had nevertheless tolerated pagan faiths, continuing the religious pluralism (provided formal worship and tribute was offered to the emperor) which was Rome's tradition. By contrast, Christianity had inherited from Judaism a monotheism which, in worshipping one universal God, regarded all other gods as idols. It was this exclusive view which had led to the persecution of the first Christians, who refused to offer even token worship to the living emperor, a mere human being, because they believed 'the kingdom, the power and the glory' belonged exclusively to God. This same exclusivity translated into persecuting zeal once Christian administrators had access to the levers of power. Both pagans and Christian heretical sects were stripped of their rights and ordered into Christian Churches to be baptized. So while there were many genuine conversions there was also token conversion. Nevertheless, many new converts were inspired by the vision of a universal faith and, making use of the network of communication established by the Roman Empire, set out on missionary journeys both east and west. By the end of the fifth century the faith had spread across the globe from India to Ireland.

Counter-culture and reformation

Alongside this fusion of state power and religious persuasion which was Constantine's ambiguous inheritance there was always within the Church what might be described as a radical counter-culture. As the once-persecuted Church began to acquire the trappings of wealth and power there arose a widespread penitent and ascetic movement which was the beginning of Christian monasticism. In returning to the desert to fast and pray, the desert fathers, as they came to be known, were re-living the experience in which Jesus had resisted the very temptations to earthly power and glory to which his Church was capitulating. Further, they were emphasizing a radical dependence on God alone and on his love which was at the heart of the Lord's Prayer and the beatitudes (see below, pp. 65–70). What began as a series of individual expressions of penitence and renewal gradually became an experiment in communal living, finding ways of being together in community.

By the fourth century there were many individual monks living in caves in the Egyptian desert. They were not centrally organized but encouraged one another by example. Their sayings came to be written down by followers and are still treasured and read by modern Christians especially in the Orthodox Churches. By the fifth century the first formal communities had been established. While the eremitic and solitary models persisted longer in the east, for the west the Rule of Saint Benedict (480–550) became the model for the establishment of monasteries throughout Europe. By the cultivation of prayer and spiritual life, and especially by the copying of manuscripts and transmission of learning, these Benedictine monasteries ultimately exercised more influence, and did more to spread Christian values and insight, than all the formal exercise of civic power of those in authority.

In the course of ensuing centuries even these pioneering experiments in radical community living became ensnared and corrupted, a development which did not surprise Christian believers who took seriously their own doctrine of original sin. Institutions whose whole raison d'être was service to the poor *by the voluntarily poor* became in their turn wealthy oppressors. This accumulation of wealth and power by those very elements of the Church which were meant to counterbalance the pretensions of civic and ecclesiastical authority eventually provoked reaction and reform.

That reaction, a great eruption of protest, political and religious ferment, gave rise in the 16th century to the third main strand of modern Christianity: Protestantism. Martin Luther

(1483–1546), who had been an Augustinian monk, wanted the Church to return to what he believed was St Paul's original and radical doctrine that we are saved only by God's gracious action and love, not by any 'works' of our own. But he also wanted to free the Church from the links with secular power that so closely bound it. This desire was widespread as many other Catholic Christians at this time felt that the Church's wealth and power had led not only to palpable corruption but also to distortions in its understanding of doctrine. While Luther achieved a formal break with the powers of the bishop of Rome, and inspired such breaks in other countries, he did not in fact break Constantine's link between Church and state. Protestant countries proceeded to impose their particular strand of Protestantism with all the persecuting zeal of the Catholic Church from which they had rebelled.

This same mistaken attempt to legislate conscience led to the flight from England of the Pilgrim Fathers, seeking freedom of religious expression in the New World. The experience of oppression, together with the influence of secular ideas from the French Revolution, led to the formal separation of Church and state in the American Constitution.

The same ideas had begun to take root in England among Protestant radicals like the poet John Milton. He argued that truth can never be defended by censorship, but flourishes best when left to defend herself. In the *Areopagetica*, his great Christian defence of freedom of speech and press, he wrote:

> As good almost kill a man as kill a good book: who kills a man kills a reasonable creature, God's image; but he who destroys a good book kills reason itself, kills the image of God as it were in the eye . . .(*Areopagetica* (1644), p.4)

Although various Christian Churches, including the Church of England, retain ties with the state and formal establishment as part of the historical heritage, it is generally recognized by all Churches that using secular power to enforce religious adherence is neither effective nor consonant with Christ's commandments to love. Furthermore, the comparative marginalization of the Churches in the developed west, and the increasing secularization of modern society, have to some degree put the Church back on to the fringes of society where it began. It may be that this return to the margins is leading to a recovery of the Church's original mission and priority, a recovery which may eventually lead to revival.

5

The teachings of Jesus

The Jewish inheritance

There is continuity between the Judaism in which Jesus was born and the new faith that he established. From Judaism Christianity inherited first and foremost the belief in a holy creator God. The story of the creation of the cosmos by God and, within that cosmos, of the first human beings, is told in the first chapters of the Book of Genesis. This is as much part of Christian scripture and belief as it is part of Judaism (and indeed Islam). Not all Christians read the story of the creation of the world in six days as a literal account, but there is general agreement among them that the story is inspired by God and contains essential teachings, working on many levels.

The first of these teachings is that the world God created was in its origin essentially good:

> 31God saw everything that he had made, and indeed, it was very good. (Genesis 1:31)

This belief is referred to by later Christian writers as the doctrine of 'original blessing'.

The second essential teaching Jews and Christians find in these stories is that human beings are both a normal part of physical creation and also set apart in a unique relationship with God and with the rest of creation. In Genesis, the idea that we have things in common with all other creatures is expressed through our being formed out of the common things of the world, the dust of the ground; the idea that we are differentiated is expressed through the image of God breathing his breath or spirit into the first human being and making them in his image:

26 Then God said, 'Let us make humankind in our image, according to our likeness; and let them have dominion over the fish of the sea, and over the birds of the air, and over the cattle, and over all the wild animals of the earth, and over every creeping thing that creeps upon the earth.'
27 So God created humankind in his image, in the image of God he created them; male and female he created them.
(Genesis 1:26–27)

7then the Lord God formed man from the dust of the ground and breathed into his nostrils the breath of life; and the man became a living being. (Genesis 2:7)

A modern reader might be tempted to read this text at a literal level and either believe it *in spite of* the way it contradicts scientific accounts, or dismiss it out of hand *because* it contradicts scientific accounts. But this would be to misuse the text. These crucial verses have been the subject of Christian meditation and speculation over many centuries. Thinkers like Augustine identified the breath of God with the Holy Spirit, the same

spirit that came upon Jesus in his baptism and which Jesus
himself breathed on his disciples – a renewing and creating
spirit which he believed all Christians received in a new way at
their baptism. The poet George Herbert expressed the common
belief that in prayer we receive and offer afresh this same Spirit
mentioned in Genesis, that prayer is 'God's breath in man
returning to his birth' (in the poem 'Prayer').

Genesis 1:26 and 27 became the locus for two key Christian
ideas about humanity. The first is that all human beings are
made in God's image. This verse became important in subsequent teaching about the inalienable dignity and rights of each
person. The image of God was understood not as an outward
and visible similarity but as an inner image, or signature of the
maker himself.

The second idea is that we have been 'given dominion' over
the other creatures. This verse has been subject of much criti-
cism, particularly from the environmental movement, who feel
that it has been used in western Christian cultures as a licence
to exploit and degrade the environment and to excuse cruelty to
other animals. While there is some force in this argument, the
verse can also be interpreted as suggesting the idea of responsi-
ble husbandry and 'stewardship'. Christians believe that we are
stewards of the earth and will have to give an account of our
caretaking to the one in whose image we were made.

Sin and salvation

Having described the original goodness and first perfection of
God's creation, including humanity, the Book of Genesis goes
on to describe an event which Christians refer to as The Fall.
Genesis tells the story of how the first human beings

deliberately disobeyed the edict of God and ate the fruit of 'the tree of the knowledge of good and evil'. The very name of this tree makes it clear that this part of Genesis is a symbolic and not a literal narrative. The disobedience of Adam and Eve destroys not only the harmony between them and God but also the harmony between themselves and between humankind and nature. Its immediate consequence is exile from the Garden of Eden and the introduction into the world of hardship, pain, and eventual death for all humanity.

This state of disobedience or alienation from God is an essential background in Judaism. The Torah, of which Genesis is part, describes how God calls an individual race of people, the Jews, to be pure and holy for him, to be cleansed of unrighteousness. They are to be a sign in the world that he has not abandoned humanity but has called them back to renew the bond of loving obedience to him, broken at the Fall. The difference between Judaism and Christianity here is not about who God is, or about our need to return to him and be restored, but about how God himself is effecting that restoration.

Christian commentators on this passage came to refer to this 'fall' of Adam and Eve as *original sin* and to trace its consequences for every human being. The sin was understood not as greed, or appetite for a particular fruit, but as pride, the desire of a mortal to be like the gods, leading to disobedience. Sin is the breaking of a bond of love, the choosing of self before God. The symbolic story of the loss of Eden, and the idea of original sin, are the terms Christians use to indicate the profound dilemmas, frustrations and evils of the human condition with which every religion and philosophy must grapple. Hindus and Buddhists might refer to the same thing as bad karma; existentialists would simply call it the human condition.

The Christian interpretation of the Genesis story is not entirely negative. The image of God in humanity is believed to have been defaced by the Fall but not completely eradicated, and therefore God's resources of generosity and love are still available to human beings. Christians see fallen humanity as alienated from its maker, and in need of rescue and restoration. The essence of the Christian gospel is the belief that God, while justly condemning their disobedience, did not abandon humanity to its fall but promised to come to its rescue, a promise he fulfilled in Christ. Indeed, from the time of St Paul onwards, Christians began to understand Christ as in some sense a 'new Adam', in whom and through whom the sin of the 'old Adam' could be reversed and humanity could be restored:

> [21]For since death came through a human being, the resurrection of the dead has also come through a human being; [22]for as all die in Adam, so all will be made alive in Christ. [23]But each in his own order: Christ the first fruits, then at his coming those who belong to Christ. [24]Then comes the end, when he hands over the kingdom to God the Father, after he has destroyed every ruler and every authority and power. [25]For he must reign until he has put all his enemies under his feet. [26]The last enemy to be destroyed is death. (1 Corinthians 15 21–26)

An originally good creation, a 'fall', and a creator God who does not abandon fallen humanity but promises to come and rescue them are common elements in Judaism and Christianity. For Judaism, the saving of Noah and the call of Abraham were the signs that God still kept the covenant humanity had broken. The call of Moses with the giving and keeping of the Law were to be the means whereby first the Jews, and then perhaps the Gentiles, might be restored to a relationship with God. For

Christians the means of restoration was believed to be both more radical and more universal. The Law was to be fulfilled not by the gradual training of many people but by the perfect obedience of one person, the Messiah. He would be the saviour of both Jews and Gentiles because in him, on behalf of all people, the broken relationship between humanity and God was healed and restored.

Atonement is that act whereby God, in the person of Christ, takes on and takes away the powers of sin and death which stand between humanity and a loving relationship with God and one another. The Bible offers Christian believers various models or images to help them understand how it is that the voluntary death of Jesus on the Cross has set them right with God and with one another.

One model pictures Jesus as accepting on our behalf a punishment due to us for our sins. This model suggests that sin itself is both punished and purged through his suffering and death, while we sinners are separated from our sins. We leave our sins nailed to the Cross with Jesus and receive, as a result of his action, a free pardon and a new beginning. This way of seeing the mystery, sometimes known as the doctrine of penal substitution or the forensic model, is especially emphasized in Protestant evangelical Churches. It has been helpful to many Christians, because it deals with the sense of guilt many people feel about their failings in life and expresses the extent of God's love in taking our punishment upon himself. It leads to a sense of immense gratitude, a certainty of forgiveness, and a desire to live a new life forgiving others.

Other Christians, however, find the idea of penal substitution a less helpful way of looking at atonement. They find it hard to imagine the loving God whom Jesus revealed as calling for or being 'satisfied' by the hideous suffering of his innocent son. They feel that to receive a pardon paid for by the punishment of an innocent substitute would be to collude in an immoral legal fiction.

The New Testament and the teachings of the early Church do, however, offer a number of other ways of understanding the Atonement. These are equally able to account for the central belief, shared by all Christians, that we have in some sense been 'saved', forgiven, and restored to love by the death and resurrection of Jesus. One such way of understanding is the idea of *ransom* – a price willingly paid, out of love, to set a captive free. Jesus himself is said to have described his death in this way:

> 'The son of man came not to be served but to serve and to give his life as a ransom for many.' (Mark 10:45)

Another image is that of *redemption*, whereby someone who has been sold into slavery can be purchased back for a price and then given his or her liberty. All these and the other metaphors that have been found for Christ's work of atonement have in common a single insight: that the deliverance for which Christ taught his followers to pray in the Lord's Prayer costs something. To defeat evil, to overcome oppression, to offer forgiveness – all these are costly things, as everybody knows from examining their own life. If it costs us personally to offer forgiveness even to one person, what must it cost God to do it absolutely for all people?

This understanding, that we are delivered and redeemed *at a price*, leads to two further insights which characterize Christian belief. The first is that the price of our deliverance is greater than we can pay, and the second is that because God has paid it for us with his own life, we have become infinitely precious in his sight and ought to be infinitely precious in one another's sight. This is the root of the universal Christian teaching about the absolute value of each human life, regardless of that individual's actual achievements or abilities or even the judgements held against them by other human beings. This is a belief which, as we shall see, has profound consequences for personal and social ethics.

The Lord's Prayer

As we saw in Chapter 1, when Jesus was asked what the greatest of all commandments was he replied by quoting two commandments from the Old Testament, both concerning love:

> 'You shall love the Lord your God with all your heart and all your soul, and with all your mind . . . and . . . you shall love your neighbour as yourself. On these two commandments hang all the law and the prophets.' (Matthew 22:37–40)

Jesus' whole life, ministry and teaching embodied and developed this key notion. Christians believe that his death on the Cross on behalf of all humanity restored a broken relationship between the world and God and that the gift of his Holy Spirit released the power of God's love in the hearts of believers. As Paul writes in his letter to the Romans:

> [15]'For you did not receive a spirit of slavery to fall back into fear, but you have received a spirit of adoption. When we cry, "Abba![m] Father!" [16]it is that very Spirit bearing witness[n] with our spirit that we are children of God.' (Romans 8:15–16)

This passage about the gift of the Spirit enabling the early Christians, both Jew and Gentile, to recognize one another as children of the same heavenly Father is rooted in the prayer known as the Lord's Prayer whose recital, often daily, is a universal Christian practice. By examining this prayer we will come to the core of what Jesus taught and of what Christians believe and teach about him.

Asked about prayer by his disciples, Jesus said:

6 'When you are praying, do not heap up empty phrases as the Gentiles do; for they think that they will be heard because of their many words. 8Do not be like them, for your Father knows what you need before you ask him.

9 Pray then in this way:
Our Father in heaven,
hallowed be your name.
10 Your kingdom come.
Your will be done,
on earth as it is in heaven.
11 Give us this day our daily bread.
12 And forgive us our debts,
as we also have forgiven our debtors.
13 And do not bring us to the time of trial,
but rescue us from the evil one.'
(Matthew 6:7–13)

This translation is from the New Revised Standard Version. A more familiar version from the 1611 King James Bible translates 'debts' as 'trespasses' and concludes with the widely used doxology (giving of glory): 'For thine is the Kingdom the power and the glory for ever and ever Amen.'

Our Father in Heaven . . .

The key to this prayer is a relationship of intimacy and trust with God as Father. In Matthew's gospel Jesus prefaces it by saying: 'Your Father in Heaven knows what you need.' This was in some respects a radical new teaching. The term Father had been used in the Torah for Yahweh, the God of Israel, but it was used only in general, corporate or cosmic terms: he is 'the Father of Lights' or the 'Father of Israel', and the references are comparatively rare. Certainly no individual would take it upon himself to call him Father personally. Yet this is what Jesus did, using in his prayer the intimate Aramaic form *Abba*.

The disciples were aware of Jesus' special relationship with God, but almost certainly thought it was exclusive to him. They asked him to teach them how to approach God in prayer, but they would not have expected to approach God on the same terms of intimacy used by Jesus himself. But this is precisely what happened. Jesus did not offer them a limited prayer for those far off or subordinate. He asked them to share in saying his own prayer. There is a paradox here. This is the Lord's Prayer not because it is the prayer he taught his followers, but because it is the prayer which, properly speaking, he alone can say, and yet he invites his followers to join him in saying it.

Christians believe Jesus to be uniquely God's son, the 'eternally begotten' whom God names and recognizes both at his baptism and his transfiguration with these words: 'This is my beloved son in whom I am well pleased.'

In Luke's narrative all this is prepared for in the story of his miraculous conception and in the prophecy the angel Gabriel gives to Mary his mother:

[30]'The angel said to her, 'Do not be afraid, Mary, for you have found favour with God. [31]And now, you will conceive in your womb and bear a son, and you will name him Jesus. [32]He will be great, and will be called the Son of the Most High.' (Luke 1:30–32)

In this way Jesus had a unique right to call God 'Father'.

Your kingdom come, your will be done . . .

There is another sense in which this prayer belongs uniquely to Jesus. It contains a perfect pattern of obedience to God, a complete submission to his will, an intimacy of love and trust which Jesus alone fulfilled. This prayer asks that heaven should come to earth, that the will and kingdom of God in heaven should be done on earth. Wherever this prayer is truly prayed and answered then the Kingdom, that is the kingly rule of God, does indeed come on earth, and the will of God is really done in the actions which are the fruit of that prayer. This is just what the disciples saw in Jesus and what Jesus himself announced ('The kingdom of God is at hand. It has come near you').

Christians believe that Jesus was himself the embodiment of that Kingdom, for he was doing and being on earth all that God wills in heaven. Judaism looks for the coming of the great day at the end of all things when God's Kingdom will come, when 'the earth would be filled with the glory of the Lord as the waters cover the sea', when wars and hatred would cease. Christians believe that in Christ the kingdom *has* come. The end and redemption of time has broken through into the middle of history. They believe that, just as in his life he embodies perfect love for God and neighbour and fulfilled the great commandment, so by his death Jesus opened a way to heaven for all humanity. For this reason his resurrection is referred to as 'the first-fruits' of a new order of reality, an order in which God's loving will is done in and through us and is no longer impeded by the old order of sin and death.

The disciples would therefore not be surprised to know that this prayer was the *Lord's Prayer*, since it testified to his unique relationship with the father and declared the perfect love, obedience, trust and forgiveness which he himself embodied in his life. What must have staggered them was when he told them it was their prayer too. How could that be? The answer to this question takes us to the heart of what Christians believe and teach about Jesus and their relationship with him.

Christians pray to the Father, as Jesus taught them, but from the earliest times they have made their prayers '*through* Jesus Christ, our Lord'. This is not simply a formulaic ending to public prayer, but an expression of the belief that being a Christian means being, in some sense, part of Christ. Christians believe that they are 'in him, and he in us', as the liturgy says. The individual prayers and petitions, hopes and desires of any particular believer are taken up into the great prayer of Jesus, which he makes continually to the father on behalf of humanity. Examples of the actual prayers he uttered on earth, as recorded in the scriptures, give us a glimpse of an inward openness between Father and Son, in the Spirit, which is going on all the time. When Christians say the Lord's Prayer they are consciously aligning themselves to the prayer spoken by Jesus. They believe that the perfection of his petition, his complete submission to God's will and his whole desire that it should be done on earth, make up for the deficiency of their own prayer and the lingering elements of selfishness and unforgiveness in their own wills. The Christian hope is that each time a believer says this prayer, joining their individual will to the will of God

in Christ, they are able to mean it a little more, to find therefore
a little more of Christ in themselves and a little more of themselves in Christ.

Give us this day our daily bread . . .

The fundamental petition of the Lord's Prayer is that God may
be loved and praised, and his will done on earth as in heaven.
But God is involved not only spiritually but also in the physicality and practicality of everyday life, as this reference to daily
bread attests.

While many Christians interpret 'daily bread' to include the
spiritual sustenance of sacrament and the words of scripture, all
acknowledge that it also means literally what it says – the food
and drink that sustain us. However we may have toiled to grow,
make, or purchase them, Christians believe that the material
goods of this world should be received as gifts directly from the
hand of God.

Forgive us our sins, as we forgive . . .

The petition in the Lord's Prayer for daily sustenance is immediately followed by a petition for forgiveness, which again
comes close to the heart of the Christian gospel. Jesus told
many parables disclosing his insight into the forgiving heart of
God, but he always linked God's with our willingness to forgive.

[21] Then Peter came and said to him, 'Lord, if another member
of the Church[g] sins against me, how often should I forgive? As
many as seven times?' [22]Jesus said to him, 'Not seven times, but,
I tell you, seventy-seven[b] times.

[23] 'For this reason the kingdom of heaven may be compared

to a king who wished to settle accounts with his slaves. ²⁴When he began the reckoning, one who owed him ten thousand talents^{*i*} was brought to him; ²⁵and, as he could not pay, his lord ordered him to be sold, together with his wife and children and all his possessions, and payment to be made. ²⁶So the slave fell on his knees before him, saying, "Have patience with me, and I will pay you everything." ²⁷And out of pity for him, the lord of that slave released him and forgave him the debt. ²⁸But that same slave, as he went out, came upon one of his fellow slaves who owed him a hundred denarii;^{*j*} and seizing him by the throat, he said, "Pay what you owe." ²⁹Then his fellow slave fell down and pleaded with him, "Have patience with me, and I will pay you." ³⁰But he refused; then he went and threw him into prison until he would pay the debt. ³¹When his fellow slaves saw what had happened, they were greatly distressed, and they went and reported to their lord all that had taken place. ³²Then his lord summoned him and said to him, "You wicked slave! I forgave you all that debt because you pleaded with me. ³³Should you not have had mercy on your fellow slave, as I had mercy on you?"' (Matthew 18:21–33)

Christians believe that to choose to remain in a state of unforgiveness towards enemies is to block off the forgiveness of God, which would otherwise be available to us. Conversely, to recognize that we ourselves are forgiven sinners is the very means whereby we can be given the spirit and motivation to attempt the difficult task of forgiving others. This teaching has ramifications not only for the personal lives of individual believers but, as we shall see, for the relations between Church and state and Church and society in matters of law and order, state sanctions and the prosecution of war.

Lead us not into temptation, but deliver us from evil . . .

It is in the context of war and its attendant horrors that one comes to look at this final petition of the Lord's Prayer, which takes so seriously the reality of evil. The line traditionally rendered 'Lead us not into temptation, but deliver us from evil' is more accurately translated 'Do not bring us to the time of trial, but deliver us from evil.'

Again this expresses one of the profound paradoxes of Christian belief. For Jesus did not personally have this petition granted at all. He was tempted in the wilderness at the beginning of his ministry and in the end brought most horribly and literally 'to the time of trial'. If he had foreknowledge of his agony to come in the Garden of Gesthemane, he must have taught this petition most feelingly. He passed through the time of trial, then came the evil and agonizing cruelty of flogging and crucifixion, from which he was not delivered. Was his prayer, then, unanswered?

Christians believe that because Jesus freely accepted this time of trial and dreadful death on our behalf, he himself became God's answer to the plea in the Lord's Prayer 'deliver us from evil'. He taught us to ask that we might be delivered from evil, but he himself knew the price of that deliverance would be his own blood. He was willing to pay that price as an act of love for all humanity, as he himself was to say: 'Greater love hath no man than to lay down his life for his friends' (John 15:13).

The parables of Jesus

All the teachings implicit in the Lord's Prayer are also evident in the rest of Jesus' teaching and especially in his parables. Telling

parables was his most characteristic teaching method. We will
look in particular at one parable in which the related doctrines
of love, atonement, and reconciliation at the heart of Christian
faith are set out :

> Then Jesus said, 'There was a man who had two sons. [12]The
> younger of them said to his father, "Father, give me the share of
> the property that will belong to me." So he divided his property
> between them. [13]A few days later the younger son gathered all
> he had and travelled to a distant country, and there he squan-
> dered his property in dissolute living. [14]When he had spent
> everything, a severe famine took place throughout that country
> and he began to be in need. [15]So he went and hired himself out
> to one of the citizens of that country, who sent him to his fields
> to feed the pigs. [16]He would gladly have filled himself with the
> pods that the pigs were eating; and no one gave him anything.
> [17]But when he came to himself he said, "How many of my
> father's hired hands have bread enough and to spare, but here I
> am dying of hunger! [18]I will get up and go to my father, and I
> will say to him, 'Father, I have sinned against heaven and before
> you; [19]I am no longer worthy to be called your son; treat me
> like one of your hired hands.'" [20]So he set off and went to his
> father. But while he was still far off, his father saw him and was
> filled with compassion; he ran and put his arms around him
> and kissed him. [21]Then the son said to him, "Father, I have
> sinned against heaven and before you; I am no longer worthy to
> be called your son." [22]But the father said to his slaves, "Quickly,
> bring out a robe – the best one – and put it on him; put a ring
> on his finger and sandals on his feet. [23]And get the fatted calf
> and kill it, and let us eat and celebrate; [24]for this son of mine
> was dead and is alive again; he was lost and is found!" And they
> began to celebrate.

[25] 'Now his elder son was in the field; and when he came and approached the house, he heard music and dancing. [26]He called one of the slaves and asked what was going on. [27]He replied, "Your brother has come, and your father has killed the fatted calf, because he has got him back safe and sound." [28]Then he became angry and refused to go in. His father came out and began to plead with him. [29]But he answered his father, "Listen! For all these years I have been working like a slave for you, and I have never disobeyed your command; yet you have never given me even a young goat so that I might celebrate with my friends. [30]But when this son of yours came back, who has devoured your property with prostitutes, you killed the fatted calf for him!" [31]Then the father said to him, "Son, you are always with me, and all that is mine is yours. [32]But we had to celebrate and rejoice, because this brother of yours was dead and has come to life; he was lost and has been found."' (Luke 15:11–32)

Although this parable is usually referred to as the parable of the prodigal son, the most striking figure in the story is actually the father. This parable tells us what he meant when he used the word Abba, father. The lost and alienated son comes to himself and begins the journey home, but it is *while he is still a long way off* that the father comes to meet him. The father's love has not changed or wavered throughout the son's alienation and exile. The son's welcome home does not depend on the special speeches and penitent status he had imagined for himself. Instead he is restored absolutely by his father's loving choice.

Christians came to see in this parable a perfect expression of their own experience of being found in Christ and restored to the Father's love. They recognized in the image of the welcoming banquet both a sign of the Eucharistic meal at the heart of

Christian liturgy and an anticipation of the heavenly banquet which was one of Christ's key images of the kingdom. A prayer of thanksgiving, widely used in Anglican liturgy expresses this insight well:

> Father of all, we give you thanks and praise, that when we were still far off you met us in your Son and brought us home. Dying and living, he declared your love, gave us grace, and opened the gate of glory. May we who share Christ's body live his risen life; we who drink his cup bring life to others; we whom the Spirit lights give light to the world. Keep us firm in the hope you have set before us, so we and all your children shall be free, and the whole earth live to praise your name; through Christ our Lord. Amen. (*Common Worship*, p. 182)

This parable also goes to the heart of another key aspect of Christian belief: the paramount importance of human freedom. The parable is based on the reality of free choice, with all its consequences. The prodigal son is free to reject his father and leave his home, but that rejection and exile have inevitable consequences which the son must bear. The father's love cannot constrain him to stay at home, nor can it compel in him a loving response – this would be coercion and domination. Love, in order to *be* love, must be freely given and exchanged. A cosmic order with love at its heart must have room for free will even when the consequences of free will may bring suffering and evil on those to whom the gift of freedom has been given. The task of love then is not to override or eradicate free will but to offer us redemption from the consequences of its abuse.

This deference to free will is equally important to the end of this parable, concerning the response of the elder brother. The elder brother allows his resentment of the father's generosity to obscure the father's love. The same love and generosity is available to both brothers, but the parable suggests that the elder brother's pride and jealousy may make him reject his father's love. He may prefer to remain aloof and in a state of unforgiveness towards his brother and, in consequence, of self-chosen exile from his father's love. The parable is left open and we may equally imagine the elder brother swallowing his pride, realizing how completely secure he is in his father's love, and from that position of security being able to overcome his jealousy and resentment.

Love and the last things

The reality of these choices and their consequences for us are what inform Christian beliefs about what have been traditionally called 'the four last things': Death, Judgement, Heaven and Hell.

The natural consequence of the sin of pride, inherent in all human beings, is to turn our backs on each other and seek only our own interests. It is possible to imagine that someone in this state of sin might so constantly prefer themselves to God that they would choose exile on their own terms rather than love and joy on his. This is precisely what Christian tradition has taught about the being referred to variously as Satan, the Devil, or the Evil One. Since all things were originally good, Satan is imagined in Christian tradition and iconography to have been originally an angel of light (Lucifer), the first and greatest of God's creatures. But he became jealous of God and sought to make a God of himself, his pride and his fall preceding (and indeed precipitating) the fall of humanity. While God's love cannot override this choice it can, Christians argue, offer a way out, involving repentance and a return to God in love.

Christians differ as to whether Satan and his fallen angels have made their choice irrevocably or whether they too may repent, but all Christians agree that repentance and return is an option for humankind, because of the atoning work of Christ. Such a return is understood as *heaven* and a refusal, a choice of self over God, is understood as *hell*. Because of the reality of human freedom, eternal hell is conceived as a real possibility. If, with their limited powers on earth, human beings can choose and build so many hells for one another, constantly rejecting the love, mercy and countless possibilities of repentance with which they are surrounded, what might they choose when they step into eternity? It may be that some, even faced with God himself, might say, as the poet Milton imagined Satan saying: 'Better to reign in hell then serve in heaven.' God's love wills and does all that could be willed and done to save them, but would never ultimately force the choice.

The parables of Jesus constantly emphasize this choice between inclusion in God's Kingdom or exclusion. Jesus often points to the paradox that it is the 'sinners', judged and found wanting by 'respectable citizens', who are most likely to ask and receive God's mercy, whereas it is the self-righteous and religious, the 'elder brothers', who are in most danger of refusing it.

The Holy Trinity, a community of Love

Christians believe that God exists before and beyond all possible worlds as one God, and yet as a community of Love in three persons: Father, Son and Holy Spirit. This doctrine of God as Trinity arose in the first few Christian centuries because it was felt that Jesus had revealed a relationship in God, a love between Father and Son, expressed through the Holy Spirit which could be accounted for in no other way.

What Christians believe can best be summarized as a story of Love – shared, lost, and found again – which might be expressed in this way:

The God who is Love chooses to share the gift of existence and indeed the gift of Love itself. So God creates a cosmos, and within that cosmos creates humanity made in his own image, that is to say endowed with being, freedom, and the capacity for love. Human beings, however, abuse that freedom and choose self-will instead of love with disastrous consequences for themselves and the rest of creation. God sees their suffering and offers them rescue by entering his own world and becoming a human being. He is born as Jesus Christ, both fully human and fully God. In their stead, and for their sakes, Jesus restores humanity's relations with God by choosing love over self, and reversing the great mistake.

This perfect love, which breaks through into the world in the person of Christ, gets a mixed reaction from God's damaged and alienated creatures. Some respond with fury and violence and crucify the God-man, others recognize him and allow themselves to be created anew in him. Intending salvation for all, including those still consumed by hate, God turns the crucifixion, the worst of human sin and violence, into the very means whereby his grace and love are poured into the world.

To complete the redemption, and as a sign that he is indeed God incarnate in fully human form, Jesus is raised from the dead. He re-gathers his disciples and sends them out as witnesses to his death and resurrection, with a gospel (good news) to proclaim to the entire world. The good news, which they proclaim and try to embody in a new community called the

Church, is that in Christ all human sin is both judged and for-given. Because of that judgement and forgiveness all of humanity is invited to make a new start, to be 'born again' and enter into a loving relationship with God and with one another which will not only blossom in this world but flourish forever in Heaven.

6

What do Christians do?

Is there a simple formula of religious practice and devotion which all Christians can follow, and, having done so, feel that they have fulfilled their religious duty? The answer is emphatically no. As we have seen, Jesus stood out against the laws and rules of his day. Instead he brought a 'new commandment' of love. This lays the responsibility on Christian communities and individual Christians to discern in their own immediate circumstances what is the actual path of love for God and neighbour, and how at that time and place it should be followed. Christians are guided by the parables of the kingdom, by the words of the Lord's Prayer, by the beatitudes (a term Christians use for the special blessings Jesus pronounced on the poor and the meek) and by the examples of those before them, but ultimately they must exercise their freedom and judgement as the growing children of God, not his craven servants.

Nevertheless, there are certain practices and traditions, rites of memory and connection, which, while not a law in themselves, are a framework in which the new life can be lived. This framework is built and affirmed by each generation of the faith. It might be summed up as prayer, sacrament and almsgiving.

This framework enables Christians to stay in touch with their community, with the teachings of their faith and, most importantly, with God himself.

Prayer

Prayer is the key. Christians believe that through Christ their prayers are brought to the heart of God and that Christ himself prays for them, in them and with them. Most Christians would acknowledge that they need daily to avail themselves of this stream of prayer, to bring their daily concerns to it to be cleansed and redirected. Prayer is both private and corporate, so again most Christians of all denominations would acknowledge the need to meet together. Prayer is the activity of the whole church and this includes 'the church triumphant', that is to say the saints in Heaven, and Jesus Christ himself interceding in Heaven on our behalf. This notion of the 'communion of saints', or an exchange of prayer and encouragement between Christians on their earthly pilgrimage and those in glory in Heaven is especially emphasised in the Catholic and Orthodox churches. When we pray we join our prayers with the whole company of Heaven, all the saints pray for us. For Catholic and Orthodox Christians, and for many Anglicans, Mary, the mother of Jesus, is the interceding saint par excellence. Her obedience, her fruitful openness to God's Word in conceiving and bearing Jesus, her words of prophecy in the Magnificat, her presence by the cross and at the time of Pentecost all make her both a model of prayer and a channel of grace. Many Catholic Christians pray 'the rosary'; a group of prayers recited and counted on a string of beads which especially invoke the grace and love of Mary, and the example of her openness to God. The rosary includes prayers to the Father (the Lord's prayer and the Gloria) but also direct prayers to Mary: 'Holy Mary Mother of God pray for us sinners now and at the hour of our death.' Some protestants only allow prayer to be addressed directly to God through Christ, but for many millions of Christians, addressing Mary and the other saints directly and joining with them in prayer for the world is an essential, joyful and comforting part of being a Christian. The traditional day on which this is done is Sunday, called the Lord's Day because it was the day of his resurrection. It is in this coming together to be the Church that Christians enter the other essential element of the spiritual life, the realm of sacrament.

Sacrament

A sacrament has been defined as 'an outward and visible sign of an inward and spiritual grace'. The two chief sacraments acknowledged universally by Christians are Baptism and Holy Communion. Baptism, a ritual washing sometimes involving complete immersion, is the rite of entry into the Christian faith and it can only be performed once. Its significance is captured in the old English term for it: *Christened*. When a person is christened they are *enChristed* – they are made part of Christ and he part of them. Another frequent image for the significance of baptism is the image of new birth. The Christian emerges from the waters of baptism born again, this time not merely a child of their earthly parents but a child of God. The font is the womb of the Church. Catholic, Orthodox and many Protestant Churches practise infant baptism, but some Protestants, particularly the Baptist Church, believe that this rite is only for adults who have come to a mature decision of commitment to Christ.

The significance of Holy Communion has been discussed in previous chapters. For Catholics, Orthodox and many Anglicans and Methodists it is the central rite in which Christian believers find their deepest unity and indeed communion with God and with one another and are given the spiritual food to strengthen them for their daily lives. Such Churches practise weekly or even daily Communion. Other Churches, for example in the Presbyterian tradition, may only celebrate this rite every two or three months, preferring to concentrate on the reading and teaching of scriptures for their weekly meetings. Nevertheless, it is still central to their understanding of how they should live Christ's risen life in the world. Protestant Churches tend to limit the notion of sacrament to these two rites. Catholic and Orthodox would include marriage, the confession and absolution of sin, and the anointing of the sick and dying amongst the sacraments.

Some Christians go further and maintain that the incarnation of God in Christ introduces a sacramental principle into the cosmos and that in any place or time God may reveal and communicate himself to us through a spiritual transformation of material things.

Almsgiving

While there is no universally accepted law or formal set of rules, all Christians acknowledge that giving to those in need is an essential part of Christian life and practice. The English word charity is rooted in the Latin *caritas*, which was used to translate the Greek word *agape*, the word which describes the love of

God for humanity revealed in Christ. Christians seek by gifts and acts of 'charity' to give thanks for having received that love and to pass the same love on to others.

Many Churches have a custom of *tithing*, encouraging all their members to give ten per cent of their income to be used for the benefit of the poor. In every generation there have been Christians who want to go much further, to imitate Christ, who gave up everything for his sake. The voluntary poverty of monks and nuns has always been an important sign to the world of the priority of God over money. At the heart of these practices is the notion of stewardship, the idea that all things including what we fondly call our property actually belong to God, that we are not the owners, but the stewards of his good creation.

Varieties of Christian experience

It is impossible to summarize what Christians do or how they worship. There is no exact equivalent of universally accepted practice, like the five pillars of Islam, although prayer, sacrament and almsgiving do form a kind of parallel. The striking feature of the Christian faith is the way in which so many radically different cultures (and indeed different denominations and individuals) find within the framework of this common faith the fulfilment of their deepest aspirations. For some it is a life of penitent abstinence, for others of thankful enjoyment. For some Christianity is a prophetic critique of the world that leads to radical action and political commitment, for others it is a mystical calling that leads to contemplation and profound inner peace.

Christianity has fired the imagination of great artists and

poets, but also drawn out and directed the reasoning of great scientists. This variety of inner experience and outer practice has, of course, had its negative side and has given rise to fissures, conflicts, and even wars of religion, but it has also helped people to build and explore a model of community in which an underlying unity in Christ allows an extraordinary variety to flourish – a kind of variety-in-unity which Saint Paul compares to the human body, whose parts are complementary precisely because they are different.

7

Christianity in the world

Politics and peace

Is there such a thing as a Christian state or a Christian political programme? This question was already in the air during the last week of Jesus' life. There was great expectation that his Messiahship would involve seizing political power from the Romans and establishing Israel as a political as well as spiritual reality. Jesus' challenging answer to a direct question about taxation has been a focus for Christian thinking on the issue ever since:

[21]So they asked him, 'Teacher, we know that you are right in what you say and teach, and you show deference to no one, but teach the way of God in accordance with truth. [22]Is it lawful for us to pay taxes to the emperor, or not?' [23]But he perceived their craftiness and said to them, [24]'Show me a denarius. Whose head and whose title does it bear?' They said, 'The emperor's.' [25]He said to them, 'Then give to the emperor the things that are the emperor's, and to God the things that are God's.' [26]And they were not able in the presence of the people to trap him by

what he said; and being amazed by his answer, they became silent. (Luke 20: 21–26)

That silence has been followed by passionate debate which might be briefly summed as follows. The theocratic school of thought says: All things belong to God including 'the emperor' and all his power. God's word, revealed in scripture and in the teachings of the Church, ought, according to this analysis, to have priority over any other philosophy or ideology and be the basis of law and civic society.

This view, which recurs in various guises throughout Christian history, has an appealing simplicity but is fraught with problems. First, any interpretation of scripture is necessarily selective and problematic, which gives opportunity for merely human power play between clerics and other interpreters. Second, Jesus' call to a loving personal relationship with God and one another simply cannot be legislated for. Virtue cannot be enforced by legal means, because you can legislate for the outer actions but not the inner heart, and it was the inner heart to which Jesus was pointing. Christian life is a journey or pilgrimage; everybody is at a different stage on this journey and will take a different time and route to complete it. To try to bring about a perfect and sinless community by legislation only encourages hypocrisy and subterfuge.

A second school of thought was pioneered by Saint Augustine (354–430) in his book *The City of God*. It was written in response to the fall of Rome in 410. The fall of the supposedly eternal city was an event which caused the kind of trauma and heart-searching provoked in America in 2001 by the collapse of the twin towers. Augustine's response to the fall of Rome was neither to take worldly political order for granted nor to deify it, as had been done with Rome. He saw the secular and the sacred realms as existing side by side, distinct but in temporary partnership. For him government is a necessary but temporary evil. While we are on earth we need institutions which will restrain the worst of our greed and selfishness. These institutions must establish such civil order and personal freedom as will allow us to live fruitful lives on earth and attend to the great task of making ourselves ready for a perfect life with God in heaven.

Because we belong ultimately to the city of God, no earthly city can or should demand our ultimate loyalty, but as Christians we should, Augustine argues, seek the good of the community in which we live and offer the insights of our gospel as guidance to its leaders. The earthly state can benefit from a Christian presence in its midst, encouraging virtue amongst its citizens and giving guidance to its leaders. Christians in turn benefit from a well-ordered state which gives them the security in which to practise and share faith. The earthly *polis* must never forget however that it is constantly under God's judgement. This view remains immensely influential and can be seen, in various forms, in the Church–state relations of many countries today, as for example in Germany and England.

A third, more radical school of Christian thought on this subject is rooted in the primacy of free will in Christian doctrine. This view insists that freedom to choose (and therefore the necessity to face temptation) is an essential part of God's ordinance, making room as it does for love. For without freedom, there can be no real love. If one partner in any loving relationship is so dominant or powerful as to prevent the other from making real choice then the love they offer in return cannot really be their own because it has not been freely chosen. So the freedom of the individual, including his or her freedom to do wrong, is paramount. It follows that government of any sort should be kept to a minimum and people left to work out their own salvation, or confirm their own damnation, through their chosen actions.

This view, which is prevalent in America and goes back to the radical puritanism of the Pilgrim Fathers, opposes compassionate action by the state in supporting the poor of society, not because such compassionate action is wrong but, on the contrary, because charity (the old scriptural word for love) is the right and duty of individual Christians and Churches, not the secular state. Paradoxically this leads to individual Christians and Churches opposing political programmes which would without doubt feed the hungry and alleviate those in prison – the very things Christ has commanded them to do. But they are persuaded that these acts are meaningless, or morally corrosive, if performed by the state and not by individuals and voluntary associations.

Because it has proved so disastrous historically (as the English learned in the bitterness of civil war) the theocratic view has less prevalence now, but the other two views are certainly widespread and can be seen shaping the politics of all those countries where Christianity flourishes.

One consequence of the development, under these various models, of Christian states and even empires, was that Jesus' new commandment that we love one another absolutely and without condition was brought up against the Roman empire's sophisticated army and the deeply ingrained militarism of Europe's pagan warrior culture. Could Christ's teaching be applied on a national as well as a personal level? Christians are deeply divided on this issue. Christianity is not a monolithic programme, but rather a series of imperfect responses to God's call to love. Jesus himself bore no weapons and repeatedly called on his followers not only to love God and their neighbours but to love their enemies as well:

> [38] 'You have heard that it was said, "An eye for an eye and a tooth for a tooth." [39]But I say to you, Do not resist an evildoer. But if anyone strikes you on the right cheek, turn the other also; [40]and if anyone wants to sue you and take your coat, give your cloak as well; [41]and if anyone forces you to go one mile, go also the second mile. [42]Give to everyone who begs from you, and do not refuse anyone who wants to borrow from you.
>
> [43] You have heard that it was said, "You shall love your neighbour and hate your enemy." [44]But I say to you, Love your enemies and pray for those who persecute you, [45]so that you may be children of your Father in heaven; for he makes his sun rise on the evil and on the good, and sends rain on the righteous and on the unrighteous.' (Matthew 5:38–45)

Christ pointed to the futility of violence and the way carrying weapons only leads to their use: those who live by the sword shall fall by the sword. Likewise, when armed men came to arrest him he did not resist them with violence and restrained his followers from doing so. His response to violence on the Cross was to overcome it with forgiving love. Given teaching so clear one might have thought that Christianity would have been necessarily pacifist from the outset. There has indeed been a consistent strand of pacifist witness within Christianity in all times, currently manifested very strongly in groups like the Quakers and the Mennonites. These groups maintain that we should simply obey the commandments of Jesus and trust to him for the outcome as he trusted to God on the Cross.

On the other hand those Christians who regard the bearing of arms as a necessary evil point out that Simon Peter had a sword with him in the garden of Gethsemane. Though Jesus healed the man Peter struck with it, he did not restrain him from carrying it. Further, they point out that loving your neighbour or your family includes protecting them. Such protection, organized on a national scale, will necessitate arms and an army. The clearest and most careful analysis of this position is to be found in the works of Saint Thomas Aquinas, who attempts dispassionately to work out under what conditions there might be a 'just war'. His just war theory is still cited and influential today, though many Christians believe that the nature of modern weaponry, and the routine targeting of civilian populations, would make it impossible for any modern war to meet his criteria.

Dealing with differences

Church history makes it clear that there are and always have been real differences of opinion and judgement between Christian communities, and individuals within those communities, over matters of both faith and practice. The first disciples had Jesus to consult, and even then the records show he had patiently to correct their misunderstandings and deal with their jealousies and rivalries. After Jesus' ascension into heaven came the promised sending of the Holy Spirit, who was to lead the Church into all truth. But the early Christians had to learn the art of discerning what the Spirit was saying to them, both by direct inspiration and through debate with one another. They had to test their insights against the precious memories they carried of Jesus' own words and those of the first apostles.

These memories, and the early inspirations and debates, eventually came to be written down as the New Testament, which, together with the oral traditions handed on in liturgy and the decisions of Church councils, became a source of authority for the Church. There was disagreement from the outset about the weighting and locus of this authority. The Orthodox gave greater weight to creeds and councils, the Catholic west to the authority of the Pope as successor to Peter the chief of Apostles, and the Protestant reformers wanted to locate authority only in the Bible. Even within these broad divisions there were bound to be differences, for the pronouncements of each of these 'authorities' has always been open to a wide variety of interpretations. The crucial issue for the Church, therefore, has not been whether they disagreed but how they dealt with their disagreements. Was it possible to live in harmony and acknowledge one another's faith, even while disagreeing radically about the practical outworking of many of his teachings? Jesus' own will in the matter, as it is presented in John's gospel, seems clear. Jesus is shown praying for his followers and their successors in these words:

'I ask not only on behalf of these, but also on behalf of those who will believe in me through their word, 21that they may all be one. As you, Father, are in me and I am in you, may they also be in us, so that the world may believe that you have sent me. 22The glory that you have given me I have given them, so that they may be one, as we are one, 23I in them and you in me, that they may become completely one, so that the world may know that you have sent me and have loved them even as you have loved me. 24Father, I desire that those also, whom you have given me, may be with me where I am, to see my glory, which you have given me because you loved me before the foundation of the world.' (John 17:20–24)

Given this prayer of Christ's, the history of Christian division and infighting is even darker and more tragic to the believer than it is to the outside observer. The mistake made by every Church until the last few centuries has been to believe that unity can only be achieved by doctrinal conformity and that such conformity can be forced on people from above. The result has been schism, and even war between groups of people all claiming to be acting on behalf of the same loving saviour. Unity cannot be found in a single set of words or formulae, in a favourite scriptural passage or Papal pronouncement, for the simple reason that Christianity finds its true unity only in Christ himself. Christ is for Christians the first and final Word of God. That word of God is not a book or a formula but a person, and the only unity Christians can have is not in agreement *about* him but in relationship *with* him.

In the last century enormous strides have been made within worldwide Christianity to heal past divisions, to recognize and act on a unity which is God-given and not manmade. This movement, known as the ecumenical movement (from the Greek word *oikumene* meaning the whole inhabited world), has shown that Christians who retain real differences of opinion about important matters can nevertheless experience together a real communion in Christ and renewal of love for one another and the world. In so doing they are modelling a way of being in a community which recognizes and honours diversity. This way is not only in harmony with the original prayers of Christ but also offers an understanding of diversity which will be essential in the development of the world in the next century. For differences not only within faiths but also between faiths must become either a constant source of war and strife or else the key to new understanding and mutual enlightenment between the peoples of the world.

Christianity and other world faiths and ideologies

As a major world religion Christianity deals with many of the same issues with which the other faiths grapple: issues of suffering and redemption, of hope and responsibility. Like other faiths it encourages compassion for those in need while calling on its adherents to transcend the frameworks of ordinary worldly experience. But, unlike some world faiths and ideologies, it does make particular and exclusive claims to be true which, at a propositional level, contradict the truth claims of other religions, however much their adherents may have in common.

For example, Christianity rests on the claim that Jesus was God's holy Messiah and that God endorsed his identity by raising him from the dead. This claim is necessarily contradicted by the element in Judaism, which still expects a Messiah. It is contradicted by the element in Islam, which, while respecting Christ as a Holy prophet, born of a virgin, does not accept that God, the compassionate and merciful, could have let him die on a Cross.

In spite of this, Christianity does in fact have very strong links with Judaism and Islam. Adherents of all three faiths see themselves as children of Abraham and as having faith in the God of Abraham, of Isaac and of Jacob. All three understand God to be a transcendent creator, the Holy One before whom we stand in awe and under judgement, but who is loving and merciful. All three faiths proclaim that God constantly forgives us and calls us afresh each day to holy obedience. For the Jew these truths are revealed in the Torah, for the Muslim they are revealed in the Koran, and for the Christian they are revealed in the person of Jesus Christ.

One might think that this was a good enough measure of

agreement to be going on with and would form the basis for collaboration and dialogue between the three 'peoples of the book', and indeed for some it does. Unfortunately, the zeal with which adherents of all three of these faiths have sought to absolutize their own faith and demonize others has led to such misunderstanding and even violence between them that dialogue has now a whole history of pain and resentment to forgive and overcome.

The historical record of Christianity in this respect has been particularly bad. Jesus was a Jew, as were all the apostles. St Paul speculated about the full inclusion of all the Jewish people in God's plans for salvation (see Romans 11). But in spite of this, from early in Christian history passages in John's gospel, which reflect the initial persecution of the Church when it was perceived as a breakaway Jewish sect, have been used time and again to justify outbreaks of anti-Semitic violence. The terrible events of the Holocaust may have had more to do with perverted science and the semi-secular, semi-magical ideology of the Nazis, but the Christian Churches could, and should, have done much more to resist them. Christianity forgot its roots and contributed to the climate of opinion in which such a poisonous ideology was able to form.

Likewise the history of relations between Christianity and Islam is, with some exceptions, lamentable. Christians might have rejoiced to find polytheistic peoples converted to monotheism, longing to honour God in Jerusalem and revering the person of Jesus. They chose instead to see the 'Holy Land' as exclusively their own possession and to 'defend' it with the sword. Between 950 and 1350, waves of Christians poured out of Europe into the Middle East to 'liberate' the holy places from Muslims and supposedly defend Byzantium from the Turks in a series of wars that were called 'Crusades'. In fact, this culture of violence was so far removed from the principle of love that the crusaders not only attacked Muslims and Jews but slaughtered fellow Christians as well. In 1204 the western Christian crusaders came to the holy city of Byzantium, the jewel of the Eastern Church and the very place they were supposed to be defending from the Turks. Disappointed at not having been able to over-run Jerusalem, they sacked Byzantium instead and desecrated the altar and icons of the Hagia Sophia, the Church of the holy wisdom (now a mosque). These violent episodes simultaneously set enmity between Christianity and Islam, and between Eastern Orthodox and Western Catholic Christians.

At the same time there was another story to tell. Just as the monastic orders had been a counterbalance to the Church's worldliness, so even in the midst of these depredations sages and scholars in all three faiths were pioneering another way. The Jewish philosopher Moses Maimonedes was exercising an influence on western scholars who read him. Islamic scholars made classical Greek texts available to the west and Christian theologians found in them an integration of theology with reason. In the midst of the crusades Saint Francis of Assisi, sickened by the violence, sought personal dialogue with the sultan as a better way forward. And in the fourteenth century the mystic Raymond Lull pioneered an attempt to find in the Hebrew scriptures and in the traditions of mystical commentary on them a common language and place of dialogue for all three faiths. These first attempts to make peace between the children of Abraham, a peace which would allow them to speak to one another about their differing claims while still honouring one another's faith, have been rekindled in more recent times. In the present political climate such dialogue is more needed than ever.

This song by contemporary singer-songwriter Steve Earle, expresses hope for peace between the three 'peoples of the book'.

JERUSALEM BY *STEVE EARLE*

I woke up this mornin' and none of the news was good
And death machines were rumblin' 'cross the ground
where Jesus stood
And the man on my TV told me that it had always been that
way
And there was nothin' anyone could do or say
And I almost listened to him
Yeah, I almost lost my mind
Then I regained my senses again
And looked into my heart to find
That I believe that one fine day all the children of Abraham
Will lay down their swords forever in Jerusalem
Well maybe I'm only dreamin' and maybe I'm just a fool
But I don't remember learnin' how to hate in Sunday school
But somewhere along the way I strayed and I never looked
back again
But I still find some comfort now and then
Then the storm comes rumblin' in
And I can't lay me down
And the drums are drummin' again
And I can't stand the sound
But I believe there'll come a day when the lion and the lamb
Will lie down in peace together in Jerusalem
And there'll be no barricades then
There'll be no wire or walls
And we can wash all this blood from our hands
And all this hatred from our souls
And I believe that on that day all the children of Abraham
Will lay down their swords forever in Jerusalem

But what of Christianity's relations, beyond the 'three peoples of the book', with faiths such as Hinduism and Buddhism? The different strands of Christianity have had different responses depending on their theological presuppositions. Some fundamentalists, tending to read other faiths through Old Testament diatribes against idolatry, have sometimes demonized the whole of these religious systems and cultures and asked their converts to start again with a 'tabula rasa'.

The early Catholic missionaries, and indeed many later Protestant ones, particularly those who learned something of Indian language and culture in order to translate the Bible, have taken a more sophisticated approach, which had been pioneered by the early Church in its encounter with Greek polytheism and philosophy. The *locus classicus* for this is the story in Acts of St Paul in Athens. Seeing an altar 'to an unknown god' he said: 'He whom you worship without knowing, he is the one I preach,' (Acts 17:23) and then went on to quote a Greek pagan poet as witness to truths about God also revealed in scripture. The theology behind this approach is that God is already at work in cultures and individuals who have not yet heard the good news of how he meets and saves humanity in Christ. The Christian revelation will come as a judgement of some aspects of any culture but also as a fulfilment of its deepest needs, a confirmation of its prophecies, and an interpretation of its greatest religious symbols and stories.

In this context the task of the Christian missionary is one of discernment and dialogue, not peremptory over-writing. Two powerful examples of this approach are the missionary work of Matteo Ricci in China in the 16th century and of Dom. Bede Griffiths in India in the 20th century. Ricci learned Mandarin and immersed himself in high Confucian culture, becoming a respected teacher of Confucian texts. Then from within that context and tradition he began to share both the complementary and the contrasting insights of the Christian gospel. Bede Griffiths took this approach even further. He recognized that in the depths of Hindu philosophy there are correctives to the shallow scientific materialism of the west just as in the Indian traditions of asceticism there is an implicit critique of western consumerism. For Bede Griffiths, the experience of India was as a call to the west to rediscover some of its own forgotten roots. Thus the missionary encounter becomes a genuinely two-way conversation.

Apart from evangelism, or philosophical dialogue, perhaps the most significant arena of encounter between Christianity and other faiths is in the field of mystical experience. Whereas there are stark and apparently irreconcilable contradictions between Christianity and other faiths at the level of dogma and creed, contemplatives from many faiths have found a great deal in common and begun fruitful dialogue. There have been good conversations, appropriately in Assisi, encouraged by both the Dalai Lama and Pope John Paul II. The life and writing of Thomas Merton, a contemplative monk with a very wide readership amongst both Catholics and Protestants, has shown how rich an encounter at depth between Christianity and other faiths can be. William Johnston, a Jesuit priest in Japan, has likewise found insights in Zen which enrich Christian faith rather than estranging people from it. Encounter between faiths at this experiential level must complement dialogue and disagreement at the propositional level if people of faith across the world community are to pursue the things that make for peace.

Christianity and new ethical issues

Since the heart of Christianity is learning to love a person, not to follow a programme, it is well placed to respond to new ethical challenges which may not have been foreseen in its foundational scriptures. In each of these new challenges Christian thinkers have sought to view the problem in the light of the twin commandments to love God and one's neighbour. But the problem of interpreting the commandments, of discerning what is the most loving course of action in given circumstances, has divided Christian thinkers and communities.

Take the issues raised by the mapping of the human genome, with its accompanying possibilities of gene therapy but also of the genetic engineering of selected or 'designer' babies. For some, the imperative to love your neighbour means that you cannot deny those who are sick the possibility of relief which gene therapy might bring. Further, if this technology allows us to discern and correct before birth conditions which would result in a lifetime of disability, then it can be argued that we are morally obliged to proceed with it. By contrast, other Christians discern in this technology another aspect of the commodification of people which is such a disturbing part of western materialism. In order to love somebody, they would argue, you must first see them as a person in their own right, neither a commodity nor a means to some other end. They should be loved and appreciated for their very being, not for their achievements on some scale of ability. According to this view the thinking behind some biotechnology undermines the dignity of the human person. It depends on the notion of 'spare' or 'expendable' human embryos. It has already resulted in the conception and birth of children as a means to the end of providing transplant material for other members of their family. In seeking to prevent the birth of children with, for example, Downs Syndrome, it implicitly judges the value of a human life solely on the basis of abilities or achievements.

Many Christians, and indeed many Jews, remembering the social and medical experiments of Nazism, see in the new technology a thinly disguised return of their programme of eugenics, with its presupposition that some human beings are, or can be made to be, superior to and of greater value than others. Whatever the immediate benefits of this technology to some lucky and already privileged individuals in western hospitals, the long-term effect on our sense of ourselves and our attitude to one another could, according to some Christian thinkers, be disastrous.

Another area of great concern for contemporary Christians is our relationship as a species with the wider environment. It is fair to say that the Churches have come comparatively late to this issue, but now that there is serious engagement many have found in the Christian scriptures helpful guidelines as humanity confronts this major challenge. The Old Testament texts shared between Christianity and Judaism have a common thread of writing about God's covenant with the land as well as with the people. Judaic law had clauses about letting the land rest, as well as the just distribution of its harvest. Texts like these are being re-read with a new and urgent relevance. The archetypal story of Noah and the flood, which ends with God's covenant with all creatures and the promise of renewal whose symbol is the rainbow, is being read as more than just a children's story. It is seen as offering profound symbols for those who care for and campaign on behalf of the environment. Western Protestantism, with its strong emphasis on individual salvation beyond this world, has sometimes neglected but is now recovering other equally important elements of the faith.

These are elements of Christianity which emphasize how all things, as well as all people, cohere in Christ, and how God plans to renew the heavens and the earth.

Modern theological movements like the Christian Ecology Network are seeking to redress this balance and join, together with other faiths, in making humanity's religious insights part of the solution to the ecological crisis, and not part of the problem. One religious value which Christianity shares with other world faiths, and which is needed as a corrective to some aspects of western science, is the notion of reverence. An attitude of reverence, of humility and awe in the face of both creation and creator, is of the essence of all the world religions but has been conspicuously absent from the western scientific and enlightenment programmes of the last two hundred years. For Jews and Christians this attitude of right reverence, which must precede and guide right action, is symbolized by God's command to Moses from the burning bush: 'Moses, Moses, take off thy shoes from off thy feet for the place where thou art standing is holy ground.'

What's love got to do with it?

How do Christians interpret Jesus' teaching about Love as individuals and as societies? The love God has for humanity, and that we ought to have for one another, is imagined under a variety of analogies and symbols throughout the Christian Scriptures. Christians understand God as loving like a parent, like a friend, like a bridegroom. God's love is compared with a mother's love for her child, as tender, all encompassing and self-sacrificing, but not as soft or self-indulgent. God's judgement and his mercy are seen as twin aspects of his love, and being loved by God involves responsibility as well as grace and freedom.

Christians believe that God unconditionally forgives all sins not so that we can wallow in sin undisturbed, but because he wishes to deliver us from sin, to set us free to repent and begin again. Christians would argue that God's love does not allow him to rest content with the sins that defile and defeat his people, however much the people themselves may want to make compromises with them. He calls human beings to purity and perfection and constantly brings them to judgement, filling them with a restless desire to make things better which has been called 'divine discontent'. The human impulse to reform and renew individuals and societies, human anger and sorrow at injustice, and revulsion at evil and exploitation are all understood to be God-given. It is God's Holy Spirit crying out and grieving from within fallen humanity. If this is the character of God's love towards humanity then the love Christians are called to embody for the world is not an all-accepting or acquiescent love. A common phrase in Christian ethical teaching is that we should 'hate the sin, but love the sinner' both in others and ourselves. The real difficulties arise when people try to interpret this and put it into practice.

While agreeing that we are all in 'a state of sin', Christians have from the outset disagreed as to the nature and relative severity of individual sins. There has been a general consensus that pride (not least religious pride) is the greatest sin and is at the root of most of the others.

How are Christians to respond lovingly to what they perceive as their own and other people's sins? The present disagreements between Christians of different cultures about sexuality are a case in point. The gospels record Jesus as speaking of the fruitfulness and permanence of marriage, and he uses marriage as a metaphor for God's relation with Israel. Homosexual practice (not orientation) is condemned in the Old Testament and in the letters of Paul, but there is no record of Jesus saying anything whatsoever about homosexuality. As to more general considerations of our struggle to find the right path for our sexual natures, what we do have is evidence of his compassionate approach to Mary Magdalene, who was believed to be a prostitute, and to the woman of Samaria, who had been married many times and was living with a man out of wedlock when Jesus offered her the gift of a fountain welling up within her to eternal life (John Chapter 4).

Some Christians believe homosexual acts to be essentially sinful, in that they fall short of what they believe to be the fullness of God's purpose for us in either fruitful marriage or prayerful chastity. They would argue that refusal to 'accept' homosexuality is itself the most loving attitude they can take to those who believe themselves to be homosexual. True love, they would say, seeks to liberate a person from their delusion rather than collude with it. On the other hand, Christians who accept homosexual orientation and/or practice would say that concern about the *outer* arrangement and gender of the bodies with which people love is trivial. The true moral issues, emphasized by Jesus, are about the kind and quality of our *inner* relationships with one another. The key question, they would argue, is not 'What gender is the person you love?' but 'Does your love engender goodness, kindness, faithfulness, gentleness and mercy?' The presence or absence of these qualities in love has nothing to do with gender and everything to do with openness of heart and vulnerability, just that openness and vulnerability which characterized Jesus' life and death.

As we saw earlier these disagreements often turn on the relation between the letter and the spirit of the scriptures. There can be no doubt of the sincerity of conviction, the desire to act lovingly in Christians on both sides of this and other similar divides. There is equally no doubt that these disputes have led to displays on both sides of angry judgementalism and hypocrisy of the very kind that Jesus encountered in his own life.

For many contemporary Christians though, especially for that majority who live in the developing world, these much-publicized debates about sex and sexuality are just a sideshow. The real challenge to the Christian way of love posed by the modern world is in economic, not sexual relations. The vast and growing inequality between global 'haves' and 'have-nots' is the great scandal of our times. There is a worldwide response from Christian pressure groups and organizations. NGOs with Christian roots have begun to speak not only of alleviating individual poverty, but also of tackling corporate sin and greed. Christian Aid, for example, not only 'distributes charity' but also actively campaigns for fairer trading relations between nations. In this struggle to deal with world poverty different Christian denominations find themselves working alongside one another and alongside people of other faiths for a common vision of justice. Thus the frontier of the struggle for peace and justice is also the frontier for fruitful dialogue between faiths, and the terrain in which the twin commandments to Love God and to love our neighbour can be most dramatically and effectively fulfilled.

8

Christianity in the twenty-first century

Fundamentals or fundamentalism?

Within western Christianity a more strident fundamentalism on the one hand and a development of newer more 'open' spirituality on the other have taken place side by side. Will these strands be reconciled in any way?

These are crucial questions for future world development. The rise of so-called fundamentalism (really a form of literalism) in all the world faiths is, in my view, one of the most dangerous developments in the modern world. Amidst the uncertainties and nihilism of western material culture a return to religious fundamentals is natural, but the question is: which fundamentals?

As I see it, Jesus teaches that *the only fundamental is love*. What passes for fundamentalism, particularly in some Protestant Churches in the United States, is really a defensive and literal insistence on one-level reading of the Bible as absolute truth. Biblical texts can then be taken and used out of context to reinforce actions and policies whose consequences are disastrous. Many would argue that present American policy in the Middle East has been distorted by pressure from Christian 'fundamentalists'. These Churches believe, alongside some Jewish fundamentalists, that the land-grabbing and ethnic cleansing described so vividly in the book of Joshua can be re-enacted today, with God's blessing, by the secular Israeli state. There are those who believe that the symbolic battles between good and evil described in apocalyptic literature (Daniel in the OT, Revelation in the New) can and should be fought over the holy ground of Jerusalem between Christians and Jews on the one hand and Muslims on the other. A literalist reading of Revelation, the most highly symbolic of all biblical texts, has led some American Churches to welcome such a disastrous conflict because they believe that they themselves would be spared its horrors by being lifted up into the air at the last minute in 'the rapture' (a literal interpretation of the biblical image of believers rising to be with Jesus).

By contrast many American Christians, equally inspired by their faith, have been at the forefront of efforts to promote dialogue and reconciliation between the divided peoples of the Middle East and elsewhere. The English mystic William Blake said: 'If the fool persists in his folly he will become wise' ('The Marriage of Heaven and Hell', *Poetical Works of William Blake*, ed. John Sampson, OUP 1952, page 250.) There has to be hope that the 'fundamentalists' on all sides will learn from history and experience where the true fundamentals lie before it is too late for us all.

Where to next?

In the light of this brief summary of Christian faith and history can we say anything about its future? The notion of looking to the future with hope is itself part of the Christian faith. Christians believe that God is the God of history, and that history therefore has a purpose. Christians pray every day that 'God's Kingdom' should 'come on earth'. Therefore they are encouraged by their faith to work for and live by the values of God's kingdom. While working to establish these values on earth, Christians also believe that the final establishment of that Kingdom, the redemption and transfiguration of all things, will be God's direct work. They believe that this will be achieved through Jesus on the day of his 'return'. Some interpret this promised return as a literal observable event when Jesus will make a bodily appearance 'in the clouds with great glory'. Others interpret it as a promise that at last his hidden presence and truth will be made manifest to all, 'and the earth will be filled with the glory of the Lord as the waters cover the sea'.

This is the final perspective of Christian faith, but what can be said looking no further than the visible and probable political and historical horizon?

Christianity is expanding most rapidly in the developing nations and among the world's poor, while it is apparently declining in the west. Will this trend continue? Will Christianity's world leaders soon be drawn from these poorer nations? The answer to both these questions is almost certainly yes. This development may restore a lost balance in the Church. The influence of thriving Churches from poorer countries brings issues of justice and development back to the forefront of Christian moral thinking. Christians whose previous religious background was animist bring back to the faith a lively awareness of the invisible spiritual realities underlying material structures, challenging the secularized materialistic culture of the west. Already the balance of missionary activity has shifted and there are now more Christian missionaries coming to Europe from Africa and Asia than there are missionaries going the other way.

Much of this book has been concerned with the nature of religious faith and relations between the faiths, but what can Christianity offer in place of the twin secular ideologies, communism and fascism, which dominated so much of the twentieth century and have now collapsed so comprehensively?

Some historians regard both these secular ideologies as in some sense bastard offspring of Christianity. Communism's sense of purpose in history and its call to struggle for justice, fascism's desire to eradicate 'sin' and establish 'order', both have their roots in the Judeo-Christian tradition. Divorced from the counterbalancing religious truth that every human endeavour is under judgement and every human being more valuable than any state or society, these secular ideologies became distorted and caused havoc. One of the most significant contributions Christianity may make, in the post-communist world, is to bring people beyond disillusion with the failed ideology to a renewal of the vision that once inspired it. In the communist east the failed experiment at a collective society has been replaced by a rampant destructive and trivial individualism as corrosive to the inner person as the old system was oppressive to the outer. The remarkable revival of Christian faith in the former Soviet bloc may be partly a matter of nationalism and nostalgia but it may also represent a critique of the secular consumerism, which appears at present to be triumphing around the world.

Faith, hope and love

Reviewing the Church and its impact on the world in his own day Saint Paul wrote:

> [13]And now faith, hope, and love abide, these three; and the greatest of these is love. (1Corinthians 13:13)

Faith, hope and love, the three great 'theological virtues', remain, by common consent, the values towards which Christians aspire and the contribution they should make to their world. 'Faith is the evidence of things not seen.' The survival of Christianity, together with other world faiths, offers us the possibility of transcending the tunnel vision of our materialism. Faith reveals the invisible reality of God, a God who cannot be bought, sold, exploited or commodified, but without whom we cannot live.

And what of hope? Paradoxically, those whose lives have been most materially blessed seem to live most miserably and without hope, as the rise in suicide and self-harm amongst the young people of the opulent west shows only too clearly. A great task for Christianity in the coming century is to reassert and defend its traditional virtue of hope, to offer hope and purpose not only for societies and nations at large but also for individuals for whom the satisfaction of material desires has led only to inner emptiness and isolation.

Finally there is love. Time and again in Christian history it has been forgotten or become an empty word; time and again it has been revived. Christian saints and sages in each generation have found new and imaginative ways to make love a practical reality in the world, to see that word made flesh. Perhaps the single irreducible significance of the Christian faith is that it has brought into the world the conviction that every person, regardless of his or her success or failure, ability or disability, virtue or sin, is equally precious in the sight of God.

What do Christians believe? They believe that for every person an infinite price has been paid and that it is the joyful task of the believer to value and love them accordingly.

Further reading

Augustine: *Confessions* (Signet Classics, 2001)
A spiritual classic, a first-hand account from the greatest early theologian, written in 398 and still fresh.

Bowker, John: *A Complete Bible Handbook* (Dorling Kindersley, 2004). An excellent compendium.

Chadwick, H and Evans, GR: *The Atlas of the Christian Church* (1987). A lucid reference work.

Donovan, Vincent: *Christianity Rediscovered* (SCM, 2001).
A Roman Catholic missionary reinterprets his own faith in the light of Masai culture.

Kung, H: *The Apostles Creed Explained For Today* (SCM, 1993).
A rereading of faith in the face of modernism from a 'liberal' Catholic.

Lewis, CS: *Mere Christianity* (Fount, 2002).
A passionate and reasoned account of the faith aiming to convert 'the man in the street', written in the 1940s and never out of print.

McManners, J: *The Oxford Illustrated History of Christianity* (1990).
A highly readable major survey.

Neill, Stephen: *A History of Christian Missions* (Penguin, 1990).
A committed and scholarly account of the highs and lows of missionary history.

Newbiggin, Leslie: *Foolishness to the Greeks: Gospel and Western Culture* (SPCK, 1986).
A groundbreaking work applying a missionary perspective to western culture.

Ware, T: *The Orthodox Church* (Penguin, 2004).
Reprint of a committed introduction and overview for the beliefs and practices of the Orthodox Church.

Wright, T: *Who was Jesus?* (SPCK, 2005).
An excellent 'behind-the-scenes' look at the Biblical material by a leading New Testament scholar.

Web resources

The Christian Classics Ethereal Library: *http://www.ccel.org/*
The full texts of all the great Christian writings of both the eastern and western Churches fully downloadable and searchable online, also access to Greek and Hebrew texts online. An invaluable resource.

The Bible Gateway: *http://bible.gospelcom.net/*
Instant access to biblical texts and commentaries, fully searchable.

Third Way: *http://www.thirdway.org.uk*
The home of rigorous Christian thinking on politics, society and culture.

The Vatican website: *http://www.vatican.va/*
Huge range of official Roman Catholic resources.

The Church of England website: *http://cofe.anglican.org/*
A comprehensive overview of worldwide Anglicanism, liturgy, history, current debates, etc.

Orthodox Christianity: *http://www.orthodoxlinks.info/*
A comprehensive Russian-based site with links to all major Russian orthodox communities and sites worldwide.

The Greek Orthodox Church: *http://www.nostos.com/church/*
Official site of Greek orthodoxy in Britain, with links beyond.

Multi-Faith net: *http://www.multifaithnet.org/*
A superb multi-faith site run by the Multi-Faith Centre at the University
of Derby. Up-to-the-minute statistics and contacts for all faith communities in Britain, in-depth articles on multi-faith issues, excellent
summary pages on the teachings of each faith including Christianity.

Index